Volume One: Reparenting Yourself

Growing Up Again

Recovering Your Lost Self

For: JAMiE

Happiness, harmony, joy and unconditional love are your inheritance. Are you ready for a miracle now? All you have to do is change your perception. Miracles happen every day.

With Love,

Art Martin

Other Books by Art Martin

Energy Medicine: The Mind/Body Medicine Connection
Becoming a Spiritual Being in a Physical Body
Your Body Is Talking; Are You Listening?
Rising from the Ashes of Your Past
Super Health at 70 Begins at 30
Reclaim Your Personal Power
Reclama Tu Podar Personal (Spanish edition)
Journey into the Light

Reparenting Yourself

Growing Up Again

Recovering Your Lost Self
Volume One:

Providing a Foundation for a Functional Relationship.
Building Trust, Self Acceptance, Validation Unconditional
Love, and Well-being In Your Future

Art Martin, Ph.D.

Personal | Transformation Press

ReParenting Yourself
by Art Martin, Ph.D.

Published by:
Personal Transformation Press
9936 Inwood Road
Folsom, CA 95630
Phone: (916) 663-9178

Websites: www.personaltransformationpress.com
www.transformyourmind.com

ISBN 978-1-891962-12-7

This book details what proper parenting is and how to avoid the conflicts in setting up a functional family. It sets out what dysfunctional behavior which causes break downs in family relationships. This book does not in any manner make any diagnosis of medical condition or prescribes any medical treatment whatsoever.

Printed in the United States of America

Table Of Contents

Dedication vi

Acknowledgments vii

Preface ix

Introduction xv

1.   The Journey into Rejection 1

2.   From Matriarchal to Patriarchal 15

3.   Communication in Relationships 23

4.   The Path to Recovery 39

5.   Understanding Relationship Types 47

6.   The Perfect Relationship 59

7.   Are You Ready to Reparent Yourself? 75

8.   Case Histories 87

Afterthoughts 115

Appendix A: What Comprises an N/CR Session? 117

Appendix B. How the Mind Functions 123

Appendix C: Body Map 147

Appendix D: Attitude Evaluation 149

Appendix E: Medical Electronic Research: The
       StressBlocker 161

Let There Be Peace On Earth

Let there be peace on earth
And let it begin with me.
Let there be peace on earth,
The peace that was meant to be.

With God as our one source
United all are we,
Let us walk with each other
In perfect harmony.

Let peace begin with me,
Let this be the moment now
With every step I take,
Let this be my solemn vow:

To take each moment
And live each moment
In peace eternally.

Let there be peace on earth
And let it begin with me.

— Anon

Dedication

This book is dedicated to those clients who had the willingness and desire to return to their childhood memories and programming that were imprinted on them by their parents and caregivers. This will allow them to grow up again and become effective adults and parents in their lives by Reparenting themselves.

It takes a lot of courage to admit our childhood was not as happy as we would have liked it to be. It also takes considerable courage and willingness to forgive the people in our life who misdirected us. They may or may not know what they did but that makes no difference. We have to grow up and forgive them for what we experienced so we can be effective adults in our lives and demonstrate acceptance, approval, recognition, validation, acknowledgement, respect and trust, and most importantly Unconditional Love.

Acknowledgments

The most important people I need to acknowledge in this process of transformation are my family. They were my laboratory, in which we set out a plan to stop the vicious circle of children growing up without the ability to trust, have unconditional love, acceptance, recognition and feeling they had value.

My clients who stuck with me over the years of trial and tribulation as I learned the process of Energy Medicine and Energy Psychology taught me more than I would ever learn in college. They were my teachers and students. I appreciate all the help the practitioners provided me to heal my body/mind and to hone and bring this process to the point it is now.

I gave up on conventional psychology in 1984, frustrated because we did not obtain lasting or effective results. I wanted fast, lasting results which did not break down under pressure or return at a later date. The process I used to learn N/CR was through my clients. They would bring me a problem, malfunction or a conflict in their life, then I would proceed to find the solution. This challenged me to find new theories, concepts and methods all the time.

Today, we have a system that will heal anything. I did not do it by myself; it took teamwork and I thank everyone who participated in the learning process. The most important people who kept our life together during the tribulations of putting our program together are my wife, Susie, and my two sons, Ross and Ryan. Over the last 30 years, our family has been through a concentrated learning experience as it served as a proving ground for many of my concepts and theories. It has proven out to work very well in our lives.

I am glad Susie and I were able to work together and recognize that we had to stop the vicious cycle of passing on to our children our own parents' behavior patterns. We had to spend some time together learning how to become good parents before we actually embarked on the path of child-rearing. We made a commitment not to bring our children up in the same way our parents had treated us, and it has worked out well.

I also appreciate the support from my clients who encouraged me to write this book. I am happy I could help them in their journey. In 1987, Chris Issell asked if I could teach the process. She set up the first class and rounded up the participants. In 1989, she introduced me to Jim Ingram. He was the first person who recognized the value of what I was presenting. He helped me set up workshops to teach the process. In 1987, I met Ken Peterson. He was a pioneer in helping me not only learn the process, but also in providing financial support to help me get my books in print, for which I am extremely grateful. He continues to be with me today as a client and a friend.

The person who keeps this publishing venture together is Tony Stubbs. He puts the books into publishable form, and is one of the most important ingredients in an author's team. Not only does he edit the books and lay them out, but he also sets up all my advertising copy and gets it to the media. I really appreciate his brilliance, knowledge and help. Thank you so much.

Preface

This book is about growing up again, which is an activity many of us will not accept as a need in our life. Think about the sentence you just read. Is this your opinion? Do you feel reading this book may help you on your journey to understanding yourself? I have discovered that most people will choose to suffer and struggle rather than face their issues. It amazes me that most people are unwilling to accept that, as a child, they didn't get the love, acceptance and recognition they needed. I've even had people tell me I don't know what I'm talking about. "My mother never did that to me. Where did you get that crazy idea?" I have posted on many Social Networking web sites, and the reactions I get are appalling. Some have complained, "Who is this snake oil doctor on our site?" "You really believe that garbage? What are your credentials?" or "Who is this freak in our midst?" I have posted my credentials along with testimonials from my clients. Does this change anybody's mind? Absolutely not! They still hold on to their fear and unwillingness to heal themselves.

These people are obviously coming from fear, and if they really faced their issues, they would freak out. At some level, they recognize I'm right or they would not react in this manner. Judgment, blame and criticism are our ways of protecting ourselves. This way we feel justified that we defended ourselves.

I find that when we begin to work in a session, people are amazed at what we find locked in their back. For example, fibromyalgia is nothing more than self-rejection locking up the back muscles, yet most people will deny it exists, even though they are in pain. When we release the pain, it is almost a miracle to them. I tell them this has roots in early childhood, that we can get the age when it happened and it's because they were rejected by their mother. If doesn't release with the affirmation we are using, then the incident did not happen. I seldom have to go back and find another incident to release the point. We always find that the body will tell the truth, even though consciously we don't want to. In the *RePaenting* process, I have found that simply returning to various childhood incidents, as I did in my practice in the beginning and as we were taught to do in college, simply doesn't work. That's why I developed Neuro/Cellular Reprogramming (N/CR) – so that we can release all the trauma and negative experiences locked in the body. (For more information about the N/CR process, see my book *Your Body Is Talking; Are You Listening,* then go to my web site www.transformyourmind.com and download the e-book for free.)

All dysfunctions in our body are controlled by our mind. Many situations that are causing severe pain are tied up by anger and resentment at parents many years ago. We find we will draw other people to us who will treat us the same way our parents did so it activates the pain again even if it had gone away. It's as if our parents planted little 'time bombs" in our mind that go off many years later so we have no recognition of when the bombs were first placed in our mind. But the pain is very real, and telling us we need to take notice and defuse or remove those time bombs.

Personally, I grew up in a very dysfunctional family. I was forced to live through many situations that caused a lot of emotional and mental pain. When I was sixteen, I was only five feet tall so everybody teased and picked on me, which pushed me into a place where I did not have many friends. When I was in my twenties, I hated my voice because it was so high-pitched. I did not know it was caused by the fact that I was still emotionally only 12 years old. I did everything I could to get my voice to drop down in pitch but nothing worked. However, as I began to address my issues, my voice began to drop of its own accord, and is now two octaves lower. I have worked with other people who have had the same experience. Everyone who has a high-pitched voice was stuck in their childhood.

This book is about my experiences with people whom I have helped in my practice over the last 30 years, and until now, I didn't feel my concepts were widely enough accepted to sell such a book. In fact in 2004, a buyer from Barnes & Noble told me at a Book Expo America event the book would not sell. As a result, I did not finish writing this book and I stuck with my book *Your Body Is Talking; Are You Listening?* However, it now feels as if the market is ready for this information as I have seen a lot of chatter on the Internet, along with working with therapists who are working with children.

When I decided to write a parenting book, I realized that most of our conflicts with our children are caused by our own childhood. Of course, I'd known this for years as a result of being a parent myself, but I didn't realize it was so widespread until I started working professionally with children eight years ago. When I recognized that this was a major problem, I decided it was time to write a book about it. This first volume talks about how we must *ReParent* ourselves before we can become parents if we want to have a family whose members can grow up and become effective, functional adults themselves.

When I reviewed the information on the Internet and read many books on the subject of ReParenting, they all seemed to be focused on going back to correct the mistakes we made with our children. How can we correct the conflicts when we are operating as *dysfunctional adult children ourselves.* Einstein said many years ago, *"You cannot correct the problem with the person who created the problem in the first place."* Unless we break the vicious cycle of behavior we inherited from our parents, we will pass it on to our children and they will grow up with our dysfunctional behaviour and do the same ... and so will their children. If we *ReParent* ourselves so we can break the barrier, our children can grow up in a functional family.

My own family was the proving ground for most of theories in this book. I have proven that if we can outgrow our own dysfunctional childhood, we can provide our children an effective model to grow up with. My wife and I were able to do so, and have ample proof in our children, two fine young men now 32 and 37 years old. We discovered that if we did not watch our behavior very closely in the beginning years of our work on *ReParenting* ourselves, our parent imprinting would bleed through, even though we thought we had it in control.

Volume Two in this series will be about how to become an effective Adult and Partner who can have children, and how to work with them effectively. I will leave you with this thought: *Parenting is not about control authority and discipline to force compliance to your rules, but about unconditional love and forgiveness.* Children want to trust us, and we must have respect for them. If you can practice the seven qualities of Unconditional Love, you will be surprised at how easy it is to work with children. If they can trust you to not take out reprisals against them, they will tell you the truth all the time. My children did because they knew my wife and I would not react and treat them with anger and discipline for doing something wrong. We always discussed every issue with them and worked out a compromise. Adult children act like out-of-control children themselves, so they in turn treat their children the same way ... and it simply doesn't work. As *adult children,* we operate from a dysfunctional parental model which causes us as parents to withhold the seven qualities of love from our children. It does not work. Children will react to forced discipline and control with defenses to protect themselves

Children need love and forgiveness, not discipline and control. We do not need authority over them. If they can trust their parents to be fair with them, they will tell the truth. Otherwise, they will lie out of self-protection, and lying then becomes a habit pattern. Dishonesty becomes cemented into their mind as an acceptable behavior because they feel they are not respected.

I have had many parents tell me their children changed their outward behavior when the parents began to communicate in a reasonable tone of voice and recognized they did not have to use authority, and stopped demanding compliance. When they began to respect their children and offer love, acceptance and recognition, thus accepting that their children had the right to talk and be heard, it changed the whole spectrum of how they responded rather than reacted. Many asked me, "How did you change my children's behavior? They never did a session with you." What happened was, when there was no need to defend and protect themselves, the children felt at ease communicating with their parents.

I never felt that way so I just bottled up and stuffed my feelings. They began to emerge as the seeds of trauma began to sprout. My body started talking but for over 20 years, I did not understand the language it was using or the message it was sending me. I did my internship, and now I'm handing it to you so you can *ReParent* yourself ... and have peace, happiness, harmony, joy, unconditional love and abundance in your life.

With love,
Art Martin
January 2008

Introduction

I never expected to be a therapist, let alone an author. But 30 years and seven books later, I feel I have served my internship. This book is about that internship. I feel we have graduated and I can look back at the path and appreciate all the trials and tribulations that have brought me to where I am now.

Working with clients in my practice has validated the original contentions I had in my twenties. I was not going to make the mistakes my high school friends made. This proved to be true, as many of them ended up in divorces with children to deal with while trying to make sense out of their lives. I was not willing to take the chance, so I dated as many women as I could for the experience of finding what I needed to know to make a reasonable decision to have a good relationship. Little did I know that I really did not know who I was or the direction my life was going. As it turned out, The path I would take over in the next twenty years would change my life totally.

In college, my major was Advertising and Journalism; my minor was Psychology. I took more courses than were required in my field so I would gain a reasonable understanding of human behavior. When I went back to college 20 years later, I realized that not much was written about this area of relationships and parenting. It is not just about learning how to be functional adults who can become effective parents and pass on a healthy world view to their children; it is about learning how to *ReParent* ourselves and unload the programs we in turn accepted from our parents so we can become a whole person. It is next to impossible to find a functional relationship and be a good parents unless we can find ourselves and enter recovery, so we can let go of the past mistakes our parents made in our childhood. I discovered this in 1992 at an Adult Children of Alcoholics Conference. My parents were not alcoholics but I felt the same way these people did when I was in my thirties. I attended many twelve step conferences and meetings trying to find out what caused these people to be the way they were.

When I embarked on this new journey to find out who I was and what my mission in life was, I also had to work with my children at the same time to make sure they were directed on the proper path so they did not have to fight the battles for survival I had to. To accomplish this, I had to sell my restaurant. To do this, I had to make sure it was running properly. I had to delegate many of the management responsibilities. Cutting loose and allowing others to help me was a real hurdle because I felt nobody could do it right except me. Hiring a night manager at my restaurant changed my life because we spent many hours after closing time talking about our situations. He had quit a high-paying job as a chemical engineer to work for us and his contention was that humans are more than just a pair of hands and a number on some company roster. People in the corporate world become robots and lose sight of who they are. After a year of talking with him, I decided I needed to find myself and discover what my mission was, and what I was supposed to be doing in this world. Up until this time, the pain in my body had gotten so intense my doctor told me not to lift anything over ten pounds, which is practically impossible in the restaurant business.

Selling the restaurant was a welcome relief for my body and freed me to focus on my desperate search to find a way out of the pain. In my search, I discovered that most modalities could alleviate the pain temporarily, but nothing would remove it permanently. This was disillusioning because the pain was getting worse. The doctors could not see any way out for me except surgery, which I would not consent to under any circumstances. Their other option was pain pills which I would not consider either.

I do not claim to be an expert by any means, but I do believe we have the experience, the methodology and the process to overcome any negative issue and help people make their lives work. We have the tools to find the dysfunctional programs and the process to release them. We have discovered how to crack the mind's codes so we can locate the root causes to anything causing conflicts in a person's life. We have proven this in our work with adults and children. Miracles happen every day because many people are committed to getting well. Some will say it is not the money or the time. "I just want my life back." Most of the time they do get their peace, happiness, joy, and unconditional love back in their life.

Where does all this dysfunctional behavior start? It started generations and generations ago. Long ago, families had large numbers of children because of child mortality statistics and the need to provide workers for their farms and businesses. Families operated with a strict hierarchy in which the father held all the authority and the power passed to the firstborn son. Women had very little to say in the way a family was run. Nobody had any real freedom, but things worked well after a fashion. During World War I, men went off to fight, so women were forced to take control of their family and run things. In

1920, this newfound power led to the 19ᵗʰ Amendment to the Constitution, which gave women the right to vote.

In World War II, women joined the workforce in support of the war machine and began to realize they could do jobs previously reserved for men, such as machining, welding, riveting and flying. They also had spending money and enjoyed the independence it brought them. The hierarchical family structure began to erode after World War II with the beginning of women's liberation. More and more women entered the workforce, sometimes displacing men when employers realized that they could hire women for less money to do the same jobs.

Children had enough problems relating to their parents before the exodus of women from the home front, but now with a caregiver standing in for the mother, increasing behavioral difficulties began to emerge. This is all on top of the fact that the parents of today's children come from the generation that maintained: "Children should be seen but not heard."

Children from the Great Depression era decided they were going to give their children everything they did not get as children so we had the postwar generation of Baby Boomers who grew up not really understanding money and responsibility. They created the Hippie and Yuppie generations, which reacted to their parents and the sixties movement by competing for status with their friends and coworkers. Many of them did not spend quality time with their children because they had their careers. Professional women would take two to four months off to have a baby then go back to their careers. This has caused a breakdown in the family structure.

We are dealing with a wider separation than we had 50 years ago with the children who grew up with no real boundaries. There is much less parental direction and influence. Some of the options have changed, with many women deciding to go the career route and not have children at all. This is probably the best thing for them to do, as children with working mothers seldom feel wanted and accepted.

This brings us to the main question: Were children better off 50 years ago? Probably not. Each generation has its challenges and it seems that conditions have not changed much. A small segment of the population does take care of their children properly and it is growing in number. Many of these are older parents who chose to wait to have children, as Susie and I did. These parents have the time and money to ensure a better home environment that will support their children's well-being.

The biggest challenge for adults is to break free of the programming held by their parents, and develop their own direction, so they will not be influenced by their parents' habit patterns. To do this, parents must be able to detach themselves from their own negative feelings and attitudes. They cannot provide proper direction for children if they are laboring under a load of rejection, resentment and not acceptable feelings themselves. That is the reasoning behind the title of this book—you must learn how to grow up and reparent yourself before you bring children into the picture.

Abused children will generally grow up to be parents who abuse their children because that is all they know. If you feel inadequate and your child confronts your fear of loss of control, you will be an abuser. It's not that people *want* to be abusers; they just don't know any other coping behavior, and are operating on the autopilot that was programmed in when they were children.

We cannot be effective adults or parents when we did not have a good parental model presented to us as children. We need to go through a basic internship on *ReParenting* before we take on the challenge of having children. If you followed the TV presentations by John Bradshaw in the late 1980s and 1990s, you can understand why most adults never grow up. As adult children, it is very hard to be competent having children. I have found that it takes ten to fifteen years after you graduate from high school to recover your lost self and get yourself established in life, ready for the challenge of raising children. Very few parents in their twenties are prepared to have children, let alone in their teens. Some people are not suited to have children at all, unless they find and recover their lost selves.

Many people have conflicting agendas about what they want to do and accomplish in their life. In the past, nobody recognized this fact, yet I often see female clients who have no children but feel guilty about not having them. This produces a body reaction in women which causes PMS and Endometriosis. If women choose not to have children, they must make peace with themselves by deleting all the programs from family pressures and religious/societal dogma that dictate that women must have children and that it is "normal and acceptable" for a women to have children. Your body does not care about what you think or decisions you make if the program: "I must have children" is in the Subconscious Mind's database. Your situation it is just acting out the religious/societal programs that have been recorded in your database. So each cycle a woman allows to pass without having a child will cause her mind to remind her that she is missing the possibility of having a child by putting her into PMS.

In my practice, it is becoming more evident each year many clients are making a conscious decision as to whether to become parents or to follow other agendas. If they decide children are not the most important issue for them, then family, church or society makes them feel guilty or forces them into having children anyway. So we have to reprogram their mind to accept their beliefs and concepts on the path they are choosing. You cannot avoid facing up to the decisions that have to be made. Ignoring it will not work.

Careers and children do not mix very well unless you can find the quality time to be with your children. When you work fulltime, it is next to impossible to provide the attention and support they need. The biggest problem we have today is children who do not feel they are wanted or have any value.

My wife and I were aware of this 25 years before it hit the media, and we decided to get to know who we were before we had any children. We reasoned that if the marriage did not work, then we would not have children to deal with during a potential breakup if that should happen. But if it was working after five years, we would be ready to have children. We knew that the first five years are the critical period in most marriages. During this "getting adjusted" period, children will take your attention and make life very complicated and stressful. So Susie and I set up a plan for our relationship and it worked well. We have just celebrated 43 years of marriage and live in peace, happiness, harmony and joy at all times. We worked hard to become good parents, and watched our sons grow up to be responsible, successful adults with good self-esteem, self-worth and self-confidence. They followed our lead and are beginning families of their own.

In your life drama, you are the director, producer, choreographer and lead actor or actress. We must know how to play our part in that drama or the play will fail. The latest statistics show 50% of the people often make unwise choices and end up in divorce. The true casualties of the failure are the children, but we put them aside and try to find another partner to join the cast of our play and fire the failed actor or actress. Then we try to restage the same play without first checking and evaluating why the previous attempt failed so we can rewrite the script so it won't fail again. Would people in business do this? I think not, their business would fail if they did not evaluate the causes of the failure, but we do it in relationships every day. Many of my clients have been shot down two or three times, then wonder why they have dysfunctional children without really digging and evaluating their relations for the reason.

The main problem relationships have is there is no plan of how to first clear up your own difficulties before having children. If you're running a business, you must have a business plan, but most parents have no plan. They find someone who excites them, so they get married. Then, for some odd reason, they confuse sex with making love, thinking they are the same. However, you cannot make love; to think otherwise is a totally wrong concept. For some odd reason, people do not understand that the basic rule in participating in sex creates babies if you are not careful in how and when you do this. Due to religious beliefs, people end up as if they are animals with having babies one right after the other with no decision-making or planning. A mother cannot take care of multiple babies without neglecting at least one or more of them.

When I started my practice, my first two insights were: About one in four (25 percent) of my clients had been rejected before they were born. I had to reevaluate my theory after about ten years in practice, because I had discovered that 75% of children felt rejected before they were born.

Take note of this: It's not what we think we did as parents. It is how the child is *perceiving* and *interpreting* what has happened from their viewpoint. The child makes the decision about how she/he feels about the situation. It makes no difference how *we* think we handled the situation. Children will react according to *their* feelings and perception. The decisions *they* make based on their perception will control the balance of their life until they can recognize the conflict. Many never recognize the conflicts they are facing because they refuse to face up to the issues from the past. I have had clients who were told to see me or had appointments made for them say, "I did not need to know that. It was buried and you brought it up ... so now I have to deal with it. I would have been better off not coming to see you." Little did they know that lessons will come up in some spontaneous way at some point when they least expect it. It is better to remove dysfunctional programs in an orderly manner than have them come up at a time when you do not want them to come up or when you have no control.

At least 50 percent of my clients did not love themselves nor could they receive love. That was my perception in the beginning of my practice. Again I have revised my percentages in the following years. I discovered over the next ten years the number who had not felt loved, wanted or accepted as children increased to *over 90%*. However, these numbers represent only those clients who were aware of themselves. The picture worsened considerably as I probed more deeply into the denial programs that were blocking many clients from knowing the reality of who they were and the programs that were running their lives. What we have come up with today is a staggering statistic; seven out of ten adults were rejected before they were born. This is not just about people born 50 – 75 years ago; the condition is more prevalent among people born in the last 20 years. Prior to 1984, I worked in a traditional psychology practice. As I found that "talk therapy" produced very little long lasting results, I decided to investigate the causes of situations I was finding my clients in.

When I began, I had no way of documenting my findings because I was moving into a new, uncharted area of psycho-physiological health. I had no guidelines to follow, nor anyone to consult about this new avenue of therapy. Many therapists were skeptical of my newfound process, yet a few did refer clients to me because, most of the time, I could break through the blocks that were stalling their recovery.

The outcome of my research was traumatic to me because I found my own challenges stemmed from my childhood, with my mother at the root of most of them. I began to realize there are very few functional families. I also began to understand the verse in the Bible: "We will suffer the sins of our fathers for seven generations." It is now clear to me that we observe and copy our parents' beliefs and behavior, and will pass those beliefs and behaviors on to our children, who will do the same indefinitely in a cycle of behavior transfer that is destroying our society. The key challenge before us, then, is to stop this cycle.

For my part, I refused to get married until I knew I could handle the basic responsibilities marriage entails, and I could be compatible with my partner of choice. I had seen too many failures in my friends' relationships that rained extreme hardships on themselves and their children, so I vowed not to make the same mistake. As a result, I did not get married until I was almost thirty, and we decided to defer having children for five years so we could get ourselves established in life. Little did we know, this was one of the most effective decisions we've ever made in our relationship. We were not able to begin creating a functional family until I decided to get out of the business world and try to find out who I was.

Over the last 30 years, I have compiled statistics on my clients, which has prompted me to write this book, detailing my findings that all the psycho/emotional physiological issues adults have stem from childhood. The seeds of future malfunctions are placed in our mind in childhood but they do not sprout until twenty to thirty years later. This is what we call adult onset illness and diseases.

There are many reasons why we feel out-of-control around children, but all of them are because of fear. It may seem odd that adults could be fearful of children when they are physically larger but it happens all the time. A chapter of this book will investigate this phenomenon. Another chapter will examine the many parental behavior patterns that erode children's self-esteem, self-worth and self-confidence.

Here are a few tragic statistics have I have compiled over the last 30 years:

1. For a variety of reasons, over 60 percent of my female clients did not want to have children but they were not aware of the program so most of them had children anyway due to family, societal or religious pressure rather than making their own decisions.

2. Seven out of ten children were rejected before they were born for the following reasons:

    a. Mistake, child was not wanted, but born due to family beliefs.
    b. Wrong gender (children know this before they are born).
    c. Mother's emotional instability.
    d. Mother's inability to handle pregnancy physically.
    e. Abusive father during pregnancy.
    f. Forced to get married due to pregnancy.
    g. Arranged marriage which did not work.
    h. Put out for adoption, not wanted or could not handle a child.

3. Many children accepted at birth were rejected after birth due to:

    a. Family difficulties: financial and relationship.
    b. Other children being born too close together so they felt rejected, etc.
    c. Favoritism by parents or in school.
    d. Emotional trauma from behavior caused by parents.

4. Four out of five children do not love themselves, and do not feel loved or accepted.

5. 100 percent of my clients suffer from self-rejection to some degree.

6. Very few people (from children to adults) know what unconditional love is.

7. Functional families are so rare that only one child in 25,000 comes from a functional family. (This is a statistical projection based on the number of people I have worked with and observed from functional families.)

8. Fear of failure and fear of success are a major conflict in most people lives.

9. Three out of five people have fear of commitment and intimacy at some level.

10. Rather than dealing with the problem, we drug children to control their behavior.

11. The main cause of all the above is that mother and father do not know what unconditional love, acceptance, recognition, validation, acknowledgment are. (I will expand this later.)

12. Children want respect and trust. Very few feel they can trust their parents.

Granted, there are exceptions where an individual is a survivor who can weather the storms, get through childhood and succeed against the odds. Some of the people were affected by their own created beliefs, interpretations, and perceptions. Even in the best of families, it is inevitable that some of a child's needs for love, recognition and attention will not be met, which the child will interpret as, "I am not loved," or, "I am unlovable." If children assume and believe they are not wanted, loved or acceptable, or if they feel rejected, the result is real to them. Their only defense mechanism is to establish the beliefs, "I am not worthy of love," "I am unlovable," and, "They don't want me," which lowers the child's expectations of having his/her needs met. So when a need is not met, the child feels less disappointment. This is a defense mechanism which gets built in so the child does not fall into a traumatic feeling every time it happens. Since most parents rarely intend to undermine a child's self-esteem and self-worth, failure to meet a need is usually inadvertent. A promise to attend a Little League game is broken because of a business emergency or because the father "just forgot." Why it happened makes no difference to the child; they interpret the broken promise as confirmation of, "I am not worthy of love, you do not respect my needs so therefore I cannot trust you." Even as an adult, he or she continues to function under the false belief, carrying all the emotional pain laid down in childhood because the seeds are there waiting to sprout.

Decades later, a person's mate may pass a remark that triggers a seed from an emotional pain laid down in childhood, which is felt as "now pain" even though it is old pain, and may be completely out of proportion to the trigger. The adult blames the mate for causing the pain, when, in fact, it is buried deep in childhood and just triggered by the mate. If a childhood pain in the mate is then triggered by any backlash, a vicious argument may ensue, like a dust devil that springs up out of nowhere in a field, leaving both parties with hurt feelings in the present. For emotional health, getting rid of that buried childhood pain is essential, but we have to know it is there to recognize it. These are what I call "skeletons in the closet of our mind," and they must be removed so they do not flair up unexpectedly.

My contentions are controversial but they work; I have proven this over and over in my family and with my clients. Parents *must* realize how easily children can misinterpret what seems trivial to an adult, and then feel rejected, unloved and abandoned. We cannot control how children think and feel, but we can provide the best possible care for them so they can trust us as parents. To do this, we must be there for them when they need our love and support.

Unfortunately since most parents do not know what love is, they do the best they can with the tools they get from books and classes or from their own experience with *their* parents. The majority of books I have read on child care and child behavior miss the mark. It is not about control and manipulation of children's behavior. It is about trust, respect and unconditional love. If children grow up knowing they can trust their parents to provide direction and support in a non-confrontational way, they will respect their parents. It is about being there for them in times when you feel out of control yourself and would act out in negative behavior, which will diminish your children's respect for you. We always have to consider how a child will perceive our behavior before we act out. Think about what you are going to say so you respond in rational loving and forgiving manner.

Careers and children do not mix. One parent must take 4 – 5 years off work, or work at home, to care for the children and provide proper attention, because one of the parents must be present for the first five years of childhood. Professional caregivers *never* substitute for parents. Adult children should not have children until they themselves have grown up and dealt with their own childhood pain. Statistics show that children from families where the parents waited until they could handle children in turn make better parents. Ideally parents will be over 30, situated in life, and with the time to provide children the necessary attention. Also, children should be at least four to five years apart in age to avoid competition for parents' attention. When a second child comes along too early, the first child feels displaced by the newborn, and interprets this as parental rejection, which becomes internalized as feelings of self-rejection. With today's stress levels, parents do not have the time to provide attention and unconditional love to more than two children. In my practice, I have found that children from large families have major adjustment problems as adults. There are exceptions to any case. We are not looking at individual cases. I am sure everyone knows about an exception. (A later chapter will examine this issue more thoroughly.)

One of the major illusions is that we are able to function normally in life when, in reality, we have stuffed and suppressed all our feelings so we can survive the conflicts of our beliefs. Our mind works well in its ability to move programs and emotional reactions into denial so we do not have to deal with the trauma. Most people form conscious beliefs that justify and support their illusions and their ability to function, but such beliefs only keep those people in a survival state, able to get through their daily routine. Many people become addicted to behavior patterns that keep them busy so that they can stuff their feelings and keep them from surfacing.

Alcoholism and drug addiction are two of them. Work addiction is just running away from the truth. There are many more.

What are you escaping from through an addiction? There are many support groups that will help a person to overcome addictions. I have attended many conferences these groups put on. My belief is they may help, yet they do not provide the direct counseling to break the addiction. We must locate the root cause and release it to become whole.

For many people, if they let their real feelings come up, they would go into depression. How do we become real with ourselves without being sunk by our emotions? This is the basic challenge behind this book. We examine the causes of negative self-image, rejection, eroding self-esteem, self-worth and self-confidence, how to correct these conditions as an adult, and how to ensure that parents do not pass these traits on to their children. According to the National Institute of Health, 3 – 5 percent of the general population (I feel it is much higher) suffers from attention-deficit hyperactivity disorder (ADHD), characterized by agitated behavior and an inability to focus on tasks.

However, they state there is no evidence that this is a neurological condition, but rather a response to modern lifestyles and electromagnetic pollution of the environment. I do not agree with that diagnosis. I can trace it back to how the parents and teachers interact with the children. Many children are energetic, creative and independent thinking youngsters struggling within the constraints of an inattentive, conflicted or stressed adult environment. Thus we end up drugging our best and our brightest children. Attention deficit disorder does not reflect the children's attention deficits but the lack of attention to their needs on the part of parents and schools. Because of the evidence that Ritalin can cause permanent damage to the child's brain and its function, the drug actually treats the needs of parents and teachers at the expense of the needs of children.

According to a recent report from the American Academy of Pediatrics, as many as 3.8 million school children, mostly boys, have ADHD. The disorder is characterized by a short attention span, jumpiness and impulsive behavior. But the study found that many cases are misdiagnosed. Most of these children take Ritalin because schools are using heavy-handed tactics on parents who may balk at the medication. When they do so, the schools are calling in child protective services to enforce their own administrative policies. If the parents do not give in, the child is suspended, which further complicates the situation.

Some welcome answers came from a man who was to become one of my teachers – Ronald Beasley. Going back over my childhood history, he was able to tell me when every significant incident had happened and with whom. The biggest eye-opener was that most of the incidents in early childhood involved my mother, which knocked her off the pedestal I had put her on 40 years earlier. I was shocked to realize that all my pain was emotionally based and stemmed primarily from my mother.

Even though Beasley's approach alleviated the pain, it was only temporary relief and the pain would always return. We knew what caused it but were unable to remove it permanently. This led to a series of experiences with clients who had the same symptoms I had. We went through all the steps I had learned from Beasley but could not remove the pain totally. I went through all the processes of forgiving my mother and anyone else who had participated in any incident, but that still did not release the pain permanently.

I went on to discover what did create all my problems and developed a system to deal, understand and release all the conflicts so I could be pain free today. With Energy Medicine and Energy Psychology, we can heal any malfunction in a person's life in a very short time. My book Your *Body Is Talking; Are You Listening?* describes the process.

1

The Journey into Rejection; Entry to the Path to Recovery

As I stated in the Preface, the reason for the title of this first chapter is that this book is not only about parenting children. Parenting is not so much doing the right *things* as being the right *person*. As parents, we must RePrent ourselves and learn how to grow up. At some level, most adults are really adult children, and are unprepared to have children themselves. Before even considering starting a family, they have to recover their lost self and find out who they are. If you enter a relationship with corrupted programs operating your mind, you will end up in a corrupted relationship. Most people cannot make a rational choice regarding a partner if they are repeating their parents' behavior patterns. As a result, we cannot even consider that we are ready to have children because we are still "infected" by our parents' dysfunctional behavior patterns.

The problem is that close to 99% of the population of developed societies do not have any recognition or understanding of the basic needs and requirements in order to have a functional relationship. We can't even consider third world societies because most of them function at a survival level. They do not even know what basic needs are, so they will not even try to meet them.

Unfortunately, most of the people in developed societies do not know what the basic needs are either. Many of us strive to get those needs but we use ineffective methods to try to achieve our end result. These basic needs, in addition to food, shelter and some form of education, are:

1. Acceptance
2. Recognition
3. Approval
4. Validation
5. Acknowledgment
6. Trust
7. Respect
8. Unconditional Love

I have had people who say I am putting too many words in since validation and acknowledgment are the same, and recognition and validation are the same. My response is I am only going with how our mind interprets the word. It uses the words in different ways in different situations. It is the same with infinite and infinity. Our mind does not accept infinite for some reason. It will only accept infinity.

All these needs must be unconditional, i.e., no conditions attached. They should be freely available from birth, yet most adults do not know what they are, so they cannot provide for themselves, let alone when a baby comes along. Most parents are so deficient in the above qualities, they do not know how to provide them to a child. Most of the time, they are being taken *from* the child rather than given *to* the child. I have worked with people who felt their mother was like vampire sucking and depleting their energy from them. They actually felt better when they were not around their mother. They did not want their mother to hug them because they could feel her energy dragging them down. With this happening to us, how do we grow up so we can make reasonable decisions about who we are, let alone make an effective choice regarding a partner?

By age four, we have lost our conception of what love is. We were born with the knowledge of what the above qualities of love are, so we begin life trying to get mother to give them to us. The problem is that she does not know what they are in most cases, so we get frustrated because we assume mother knows what love is. Since we were born with love, we continue trying to get her to give it to us. Since she does not know why we are acting out and crying, she gets upset and irritated. Many times, this turns into verbal or physical abuse. Since children cannot get the desired result of recognition, acceptance and love, they tend to resort to getting sick so mother will have to take care of them. Many of the behavior patterns adults have are hatched in the first five years of life. (We will go into those later in the book.)

Why is it so important that parents be the right people and not just say and do the right things? We have to be authentic and walk our own talk. Children are very intuitive and can see right through the games and fronts we put up, even if we do not know we are putting up a false front. They react to *their perceptions*, not what we want them to see. This is why it is so very important to *ReParent* ourselves. If we want to be successful in our outer world, we have to be real. Who we present to the outer world is like radar, in that the person we are talking to will actually make a decision as to who we are before we speak a word. Everybody is sizing up everyone they meet before they communicate. This is meta-communication. Unfortunately we are not listening to the inner self's communication; instead, we are listening to our judger conscious mind's feedback which is inaccurate most of the time because we can only judge based on our own interpretations of who we are. In other words, we are filtering through our distorted view of who we think we are. Once you are in control of your mind and have the judger out of the pattern, you can make accurate interpretations of the sensory feedback you are receiving

Many surveys about what adults remember from their childhood reveal that people remember what happened in positive events. They tend to block and stuff their negative experiences. I have discovered almost all negative experiences are locked up in denial. This is our mind's way of blocking us from having to revisit these events. Our memory is still intact, but our mind has successfully blocked them so we do not have to remember them. We are most heavily influenced by our parents' characteristics and their behavior patterns rather than their words. It is our demonstration of who we are that influences children's behavior. Children learn by example, which means we have to be on our good behavior 24/7 when we are around them. Children do not let anything slip by; they are observing all the time. You do not need to say anything at all to influence them. They are picking up your thoughts and feelings along with all the events and experiences you have in front of them. Even if you try to cover up or block situations from them, they know what happened and will react to it. Their intuitive ability is extremely sharp until about seven years old. Unfortunately education, parents and peer group pressure tend to block our intuitive ability as we grow up. Some adults retain the ability, plus it can be rebuilt without too much effort.

A case in point: a young man came in with this complaint: "I can't trust women, even though many of them are attracted to me. I seem to get into relationships that eventually fall out. It is not hard to get into relationships and in fact many of them are great experiences but something always comes up to cause them to fail. Why?"

We discovered after a few sessions that when he was four years old, his mother had an affair which she covered up very well. When his father found out, he tried to block the children from finding out what was causing disruption in the relationship. My client knew consciously something was wrong in the family but he never knew it was the affair because it was not discussed openly. Even though he did not know what was causing his mistrust of women, it was a very active program in his mind. When he forgave his mother and released all the conflicts in his mind about being rejected by his mother, we were able to reinstall a new program that would allow him to trust women. It is a long story that came to a successful conclusion because he was willing to dig into the conflict in his mind. His role model failed in her responsibility to show him he could trust her.

During the first seven years of life, children are desperate for role models to show them how to be, how to interact with the world, how to ensure their survival and how to deal with conflict. The examples set by those closest to them, their parents and older siblings, are remembered as the single most potent source of guidance about how to behave. It is therefore imperative that the primary caregivers, usually the parents, offer role models that embody self-love, self-approval, self-esteem and a sense of self-worth. They should also possess and pass on a solid set of values, ethics, and moral standards.

In addition to modeling personhood, parents also model relationship skills ... or lack of them. The classic two-parent family with a healthy, functional relationship is a powerful model from which children learn how to have adult relationships themselves. Unfortunately, most young adults (and potential parents) are operating with self-negating programs inherited from childhood. So, again we must *ReParent* ourselves before we venture out into relationships.

Fewer than half the families in the United States are headed by two parents, and less than five percent of those are functional enough to prepare young adults to enter into functional relationships and effectively raise children of their own. To create a functional family ourselves, we must grow up and *ReParent* ourselves. We must release all the parental programs that were installed during our own childhood. If we enter into relationships without unloading this inherited garbage, we will seek out a partner who matches our dysfunctional needs. We will treat our children the same way we were treated. However, few couples spend the time planning and organizing their lives, or undergoing relationship and parenting counseling so that they can form a functional family. How do we make right and positive choices so we do not end up in the relationship garbage dump trying to dig our way out? That is what this book is about. If we follow the directions, we can find a functionally effective relationship that contains unconditional love and all six other basic qualities that love forms around. If you do not clear up the skeletons in the closet of your mind they will surely begin rattling at some point in your life and cause breakdowns or meltdowns in relationships, your career and your body. There are many examples in the news every day, such as tragic murder/suicides.

Even though Susie and I committed to not treating our children the way we had been treated, and then waited six years before our first son was born in 1971, our parents' behavior still tried to sneak in all the time. By the time our second son was born five years later, we had the parental programming under control but still had to watch our behavior very closely. By 1979, we had finally mastered the parental issues that had caused us problems.

I have worked with hundreds of clients where we have retrospectively had to deal with parental issues. With many, the damage had already been done to their children, so they had to release the guilt and try to make peace with their children as soon as possible. For many, regaining their adult children's trust took a long time. Most people do not recognize the need to reparent their children when they become aware they did not provide the proper parenting model in the beginning. We must go back and correct the mistake we made with them. It may seem as if they do not want to work with us at first because they do not trust or respect us; we must gain their respect and trust. We cannot do this until we reparent ourselves and grow up again. We must have the courage to confront our own dysfunctional behavior before we can change our children's behavior. This is best done before we get into committed relationships and definitely before we have children. If you did not have that awareness, can you recognize the need to make the choice now? If you are in a relationship, it is time to take stock of where you are now in your life and get on the track to reparenting yourself before you have any further conflicts and problems. If your first or second attempt to put together a functional relationship did not work, it is definitely time to take an inventory on the challenges you are facing.

Most relationships that did not work are caused by looking for love in the wrong places. A relationship never starts with love. It takes years to work into a love relationship. It takes a lot of compromise and communication. Unfortunately people have children long before they are ready to provide their children a stable family life. It will create conflicts in a relationship so couples cannot get situated in a manner where they can accomplish an effective relationship.

If we cannot provide a functional relationship between ourselves as parents, how do we expect to bring children into this world when we do not know what the seven qualities of love are? If we cannot apply them to our own relationships, how do we expect to apply them to children? Most of us are self directed in such a way we are looking out for our own best interests and will reject or refuse to see the need to communicate and cooperate to create a functional relationship. Are we going to bring children into our dysfunctional world? Most of us do not even consider this.

We must reparent ourselves long before we consider bringing children into our relationship. Susie and I knew we could not function in a rational manner with children, let alone ourselves, until we found ourselves and came to a point of understanding on how we would deal with children in a rational, functional manner. We spent almost six years in the process of reparenting ourselves. We did not describe it in that manner at the time even though this is what we were doing. We attended many workshops and seminars on personal growth to understand where we were and what direction we had to take to create a functional relationship. Many times it was rough to face the issues we had to overcome on our path. We could have ended up in divorce at least two times when the going was tough to face but we did not stray off the path. When we made mistakes we confronted them. Many people would have just given up and ran out blaming the partner as an excuse to breakup. Quite often people will change partners but not change the script they operating with so they draw the same person in. The only situation that changes is the name.

What do you do at this point? We knew if you do not face the lesson and deal with it now the lesson will come up again and again until we face the issue. However, each time a lesson comes up it escalates and gets more intense. It may involve different people with different names, but the lesson with be the same. Running away from the issue does not solve anything you have work out the issue before you depart. Sometimes it can be worked out and other times two people have to separate once they overcome the lesson. You cannot divorce the lesson; it will keep chasing you.

If it gets to the point where you have to work out issues with children present, you have much more complicated issue. The children have their own impressions and perceptions which may not be accurate but you have to work with them too.

The challenge was first to get their children to see their parents' mistakes, and then work to rectify the issues before they got any worse and were passed on to the next generation. Resentment was one of the biggest issues, and one of the hardest things to let go. You can not Reparent children until you Reparent yourself. You cannot give what you do not have. Children know that and will not allow you to work with them until you have the ability to set up trust and respect for them. When they feel they can trust you they will venture out of the shadows and let out their feelings. It is amazing how easy it is to work with children who are not holding on to resentment and anger.

Many times, a client would bring in three generations of family to see me so that we could stop the vicious cycle of negative programming before it got out of hand and spread to a fourth generation. Working on family issues with hundreds of people has reinforced my contention that we must stop this legacy of parental behavior transfer before it gets any worse.

In addition to modeling functional behavior and relationship skills, parents need to establish consistent boundaries on their children's behavior, with clearly defined consequences for breaching a boundary. Managing domestic discipline fairly and without confusing who the child *is*, versus what the child *does*, takes maturity and thoughtfulness on the part of parents.

Children are not what they do. Who they are is not their behavior. We all make mistakes. The mistake is not who we are. It is an action which needs to be discussed. It is very hard for parents to separate an issue from the child. Their behavior is goal-oriented; they have one end result—attention or recognition. Very few parents see this as an end result because they are operating from the control, authority, discipline and compliance model. It does not work and never has even though this is the model most people were brought up with.

Unfortunately most child rearing books promote this program. Many books have been written by well known and accepted authors. I differ with them because I have discovered a parenting program which works without a glitch. The children trust and respect their parents and they are happier, more successful children. They recover their self esteem, self worth and self confidence. They do better in school and there are no discipline problems to deal with.

Many parents threaten children with punishments that cannot be carried out, which erodes the child's respect for, and relationship with, the parent. Children's respect and honor for their parents is essential to good discipline, so that the children avoid behavior that would erode their relationship with the parents. But, in many families, do parents strive to earn their children's respect, and do children strive to earn their parents' respect? It is hard to do if you did not start out with a functional behavior pattern as babies.

How do we stop history from repeating itself? People have been handing down their negative habit patterns to their children and repeating their parents' behavior for centuries. How do we expect to create an effective and functional family atmosphere when we repeat the same mistakes our parents made?

Most cultures and societies have different levels of negative behavior passed down through the generations. This is why hatred proliferates in many countries; it has become so ingrained in the culture that people have no idea how to accept those who are different or how to forgive those who transgress. An act of terrorism is met by a retaliatory attack, which is escalated by more terrorism, and so on, until the last person standing is declared the winner. This is what is happening in the Middle East as each new generation is born into hatred. Love does not exist in such societies, as hatred is passed down through the generations from ancient times.

In the western world, the dysfunction in family behavior is not as serious as in underdeveloped countries, but still causes major crises in many families. Why does this continue to happen when we are increasingly aware of our difficulties in communication? It may seem we are becoming more educated on behavioral difficulties, but my work with clients over the last thirty years does not show this happening. My experience overall indicates to me people hunkering down and digging in deeper to escape their fears and feelings of loss of control of their lives. What type of a model does this show our children? If we cannot deal with societal stress, how are *they* going to, if we do not provide a functional model?

We may be revisiting the living conditions that happened during the 1930s Great Depression Era, since we have the conditions present today which may cause a depression. We have three generations of people who have never lived in a time of want and need. How will they handle the stress? We are confronted with a similar situation under new conditions. What will be the outcome? We will have to wait and see.

When researching the root causes of behavioral malfunction, we must look at history. Psychology is a relatively young science and, even though the philosopher Descartes proclaimed in 1654 that the body and mind are two entities, modern psychology can trace its origins back to Freud. Since then, some philosophers have mixed philosophy with human behavioral science. In reality, modern psychology is only about 100 years old, and any real understanding of human behavior began with Carl Jung. There have been many schools of thought within psychology over the past 100 years, yet my experience over the last thirty years shows me we have really only just cracked the surface in coming to an understanding of human behavior. We have learned more in the last ten years than we have in the last 100 years. Much of the brain/mind/body connection is just becoming understood now. This is what my research has been about for the last thirty years.

2

From Matriarchal to Patriarchal

From the days of ancient prehistory to early agrarian cultures (about 7000 BC), the Earth and Nature ruled people's lives completely through the annual fertility cycle of the seasons. It was natural for people to project the forces at work onto an external deity. In years of bountiful harvest, the projection, the Great Mother, was believed to be pleased with Her children, and lean years and natural disasters such as earthquakes and floods were taken of signs of Her displeasure. Figuring that something they had done had displeased their deity, they strived to regain Her good graces, which is the origin of organized religion's claim that God expects us to behave in certain ways in order to win His approval.

In early matriarchal cultures, the Mother Goddess was always symbolized as a pregnant woman, and childbirth was seen as a gift, with women revered as its recipients in some mysterious conspiracy that men feared. As the Bronze Age gave way to the Iron Age about 1250 BC, small tribes were joining into larger groups, so conflicts between groups meant traveling longer distances to wage war. This precluded women, who had to stay in their villages with the children. As the spear replaced the plow in authority, specialized armies, exclusively male, were formed, and began to project such noble human qualities as courage and aggression onto male deities that they created. The cultures of patriarchal warriors formed the basis of the Old Testament's male deity, and began to suppress the ancient goddess-based religions, such as the cults of Isis and Astarte. Women lost their "revered status" and became second-class citizens, attributed with the "dark side" of humanity, a status that Christianity and Islam have reinforced for 2,000 years ... and still do.

For example, in the Middle Ages, the Roman Catholic Church killed an estimated nine million people – put them to the sword, burned them at the stake, or stoned them to death. Most of them were women, who were frequently tortured in sexually deviant ways by the supposed celibate priests as a way to out-picture their fear of the feminine side of human nature.

Christianity is not alone, of course. Judaism and Islam both relegate women to second-class status and list situations when she is "unclean" and must not handle food, and stipulate how many steps a good wife should walk behind her husband. This has been a typical pattern in Asian cultures, too.

So historically, ours has been a patriarchal society for many millennia, in which women and children were considered chattel property of the controlling male. Larger families meant more field workers, more sons to sell into the church as priests and more daughters to become nuns, or to the military as soldiers, which gave patriarchs a higher political standing in the community. Women had – and still have – no rights and little value in many cultures except for their ability to bear children, provide sexual pleasure and keep house.

I can remember, when I was a teenager in the fifties, one of my friends telling me goodbye because he was being sent to a seminary to become a priest. He had no choice or any right to object. Neither did two of his older sisters, who were sent to convents. I can remember his parents extolling the virtues of their three children who "chose" to serve the church. It was a false claim and all the children in the neighborhood knew it.

In the United States, World War I saw a change in family structure when women often had to take over running the family in the men's absence. After World War I, during which women had acted as the head of many households, they finally got the vote in 1920. The Great Depression brought more pressure on the male-dominated culture as many women were stronger than their husbands in keeping the family together during the crisis. World War II brought many women back into the workforce, where they took jobs formerly held by men, such as those in shipbuilding. This brought about a major shift in the societal structure, as women were accepted into the working society.

At the end of the Second World War, people began to see they could now provide luxuries to their families they were not able to afford during the Depression. Many parents began to give their children everything they did not get as children. Out of guilt, they would go overboard with gifts and buy anything their children wanted. They were going to provide their children with all the things they did not have, which caused a loss in personal value.

These children now form the Baby Boomer generation, who began to move out of the central cities to the suburbs. The pressure was on to keep up with the Jones', and two cars began to show up in the garages of the increasingly larger houses. The economy was good, there was no inflation, and the dollar went a long way. Lack of pressure for two income families allowed many women to stop working and go back to being homemakers. Some women did not go back, however, and began to work in many job positions that were never available to them before the war.

This was the start of the women's movement for equality. The late 1950s were boom years for the United States, and everything seemed rosy in our world. Between the Korean and Vietnam Wars, women began to enter the work force, as jobs were plentiful and the economy was expanding dramatically. In the 1960s, for the first time, courtesy of the nightly TV news, the American public was placed on the battlefields of the Vietnam War, and saw the horror and carnage of warfare. Many young men refused to answer the draft – something unthinkable in WW II and the Korean War. As they began to react against their parents' world and go against the cultural rules of the past, the climate shifted. They were no longer passive and followed their consciences, which created a major cultural revolution. At the same time, more women began to go to college and enter fields traditionally held by men, such as science, engineering and medicine, and many other professions and jobs. In the 1970s, the Baby Boomers became parents and spawned the "I-me" Generation-X, or the Yuppies. These children began to look at life as if the world owed them a living.

When inflation began to set in, people found they could no longer get by on a single income and still satisfy their appetite for the luxuries of the new lifestyle. As a result, women began to move from full-time mothering to part-time mothering as they entered the work force. The 1960s were the turning point; "latch-key kids" were unheard of before the 1970s.

As more people placed personal fulfillment and self-realization ahead of their children's needs, the divorce rate skyrocketed. In the past, couples had stayed in a relationship for the children or because of religious and parental pressure, but this began to end. Falling church attendance and the break-up of the extended family due to population mobility further eroded these traditional pressures. Also, for the first time, women had their own income so were no longer financially dependent on men for their survival.

The 1970s pressure on two-income families forced more women into the workforce. However, as they began to be a moving force in business and politics, the male-dominated business world felt threatened. A male backlash occurred amongst men who were afraid of losing their power. The shift of power had many insecure men upset about losing their illusion of superiority, which caused them emotional and physical dysfunction, evidenced by the increase in the number of prostate cancer cases among men feeling emasculated by women taking their power. This phenomenon had never been experienced in the past.

With the erosion of cultural values in the 1980s, 1990s and 2000s, we now have the so-called Y-Generation aged 18 – 25 in 2009, a generation of young people who do not seem to have many values nor do they feel they have a future. Although there are exceptions, they tend to be totally self-absorbed, and cannot relate to causes larger than themselves, such as patriotism. In the last five years, six of my sons' friends have died, two of them from unknown causes, one from a heart attack at only 24 years old, one from drowning and one by suicide. Young people's music also indicates their despair.

Most of this Y-Generation hopelessness can be attributed to one fact: that few children had a full-time mother when they were growing up. Statistics also reveal that over fifty percent of today's children live in single-parent families. Many of these parents are in the business field and have long commutes, so they see very little of their children. Long working hours and long commutes mean they cannot spend quality time with their children, so TV and video games have become the modern baby-sitter, even when the parents *are* home.

One of my clients works as a nanny for a busy dot-com executive. She takes care of the children during the day, and a live-in housekeeper takes care of them at night. The children have begun to call my client "Mom" because she is with them much more than the parents are. She takes them to school and picks them up, takes them on trips, outings and does the grocery shopping and takes them to the shopping mall to buy clothes, etc. They have even told her they like her better than their mother. What does this tell us? Children feel the parents don't care. They do not fit in to their parents lives. Such casea involve couples who should not have had children.

Another case in point: I had a couple come to see me during the big expansion in the computer industry in the early 1990s. They had everything going for them. They seemed to be functional parents; they had wealth to provide a great life for a child and took all the right actions for the first four years of their child's life. They built an 8,000-square-foot house with the children's quarters at one end with accommodations for a nanny, and the parents' rooms were at the other end. They had a large play room with carpet on the walls and all the toys, etc., imaginable. The mother took time off work, going to work one day a week and stayed home with their son. When he was four, they enrolled him in a very expensive pre-school and hired a nanny to take care of him. Unfortunately, just before the son was five, he died of undisclosed causes. The autopsy could find no cause of death, so was described as Sudden Infant Death Syndrome (SIDS). When I took a look into the situation, we discovered that the boy was very sensitive and intelligent, which was verified by the school. Yet, he felt rejected and alone. His mother was no longer able to be with him, so he felt she did not care because she had provided perfect care for the first four years, then abruptly left him. This was his perception, of course. The nanny was a housekeeper and a cook, too. She did not have a good relationship with the boy like the prior case. She did not replace the mother's attention. So, he did not see his mother very often. They did not want to have another child for fear there was some genetic defect they were carrying. However, this was disproved in medical tests. The real cause of death was the mother's abrupt rejection with no explanation for the child to understand. If she had shifted back to work slowly by working one more day a week for about six months, the outcome may have been different.

3

Communication in Relationships

When children feel their parents no longer care for them, then of course, we'll have problems with them, such as depression, delinquency, and suicide. Now, most parents want to take care of their children and many of them do, but the rest have conflicting agendas in which the children have a lower priority. Also, the parents never learned parenting skills, which includes knowing how to communicate with their children.

Working with Adopted Children

With western customs invading Eastern Europe, there have been many children born to single mothers who do not want them. It is almost as if they do not know what the fun of sexual relationships produces. We have many children who end up in orphanages, and many of these children are being adopted by families in the US. It is a great concept but if the parents are not ready to deal with an adopted child who was rejected by his/her birth mother, and then spent time in an institution where there were no parents, they have an eye-opening experience in front of them.

These children have been subjected to major rejection and abandonment, and the trauma is intense for them to overcome. As a result, most of them will react to anybody trying to get close to them. They will push the adoptive parent away because they do not trust them. If you have been through as much rejection as they have, their perception is, "I was rejected in the past, so why should I trust this person who may do it again."

The adoptive parents do not understand how the mind functions so they may try to force the issue, which makes it worse. They try to use the dysfunctional parenting program of control, authority, discipline and compliance and just make behavior problems worse.

These are special cases that require a lot of understanding and unconditional love. If you do not know what love is, the children will not allow you to get close to them. Most of them have Radical Associative Disorder or, as I would rather call it, Radical Attitude Disorder. I know they are disassociating but it is really their *attitude* that causes the dysfunction.

When I have worked with these children, I find I can get them back on track in a session or two. All you have to do is allow their mind to recognize that they *can* let go of their irrational fear by forgiving their birth mother and all the people who mistreated them in the past. Once you do that, they can release all the resentment and fear of intimacy and commitment blocking their ability to trust and accept love.

When you have been through a series of traumatic experiences it is very hard to accept it is not going to continue. What these children need is unconditional love, recognition and acceptance. They are dealing with major issues about value. They see themselves as having no value; this why they have been thrown around in their interpretation. We can not look at this rationally. We have to see it through their eyes. *Again take note of this:* it is not how we see it; it is how the child perceives it which creates his/her interpretation.

Children will always see issues based on their past experience because their mind can only make sense of what they know and then project it into the issue at hand. As a result most adopted children, from a local adoption agencies or from off shore agencies have similar behavior patterns. They are focused on three fronts: safety, security and protection. They do not feel safe with a family they do not understand yet. They do not feel secure in a place where they don't know what will happen. They do not feel protected, no matter what an adopted parent does to assure them they are caring for them. In most cases, they will not allow the adoptive parent to get close to them until they feel they can trust them. The main conflict is that most people do not know what love is. So how do you try to provide something which you do not have within you? This is a major conflict that causes many problems for adoptive parents. Again one should have gone through a reparenting process so that children can know they are accepted and loved. You can't do this if you do not have a love program installed in your mind.

Many people who adopt these children have no basic concept about parenting to begin with, so they have an uphill battle. They usually cannot produce children so they are needy in their desire to have children. They want children desperately so they are shocked and upset when the child rejects them. If the adoptive parents are functioning out of fear programs themselves, they will project this fear to the child.

Adopting a child from our own society presents the same challenges since the child was rejected by his/her birth parents. This is the worst form of rejection. Children have an amazing bond with birth parents no matter what happened, and while this cannot be broken, we can allow the adoptive parents to make a new bond with the child that will work if they know what love is.

(For more information on these concepts about conflicts with adoption and dealing with RAD disorders or to purchase the books and CDs by Heather Forbes, check references at back of this book or go to: www.beyondconsequences.com.)

The major conflict is communication ... or lack of it. Parents do not have the time or patience to spend quality time with their children, which is vital for a child to feel valued and worthy. There is also the false cultural belief that caring for children is women's work. Some men feel that all they need to do is support the family, and leave the family chores to the women ... and children are often seen as a chore. Now that more women are working, the couple must share the responsibilities, but that often does not happen. Many of my female clients complain about having to work all day, then go home and start the second shift. Between the household chores and basic (not quality time) care of the children, they have no time for themselves. Such stressed mothers are prone to negative behavior toward the children and possibly depression. And quite often, the outcome is divorce ... with custody usually going to the mother. Then, she is even more isolated from the father's support, as his involvement with the children is often limited to a couple of weekends a month. Her only recourse is daycare for preschoolers, and after-hours care at school for those not old enough to become latchkey kids. When she gets home later, exhausted, quality time with the children is out of the question, so they grow up feeling unwanted, not respected, and not listened to as adults. Of course, women's rights organizations defend mothers' entitlement to a career and a fulfilling life outside the home, and society bends over backwards to be politically correct, and lends its approval. And a new generation of dysfunctional parents-to-be goes forward into the future.

So where do we go when this happens to us as children? We have to work out all the conflicts and problems that created our dysfunctional behavior. But first we must recognize that we are carrying these behavior patterns. Sometimes it is difficult to be willing to accept this pattern in your life. If you do not have peace, happiness, harmony and joy with unconditional love in your life, you need a review and rework of your behavior patterns. This is what I have developed over the last thirty years – a method to change your life and rewrite the scripts in your subconscious mind's database so you can have the qualities that will create happiness and well-being in your life.

To illustrate these behavior patterns, here is a typical case of a man who, trying to cling on to his power and control, reacted violently: I was at a friend's home discussing a business proposition. When we had finished, his wife asked me if I had time to do a session with her, which I did. During the session, her husband burst into the room to tell us that their son had pooped in his diaper. She replied, "We're busy. Can you change him?"

He replied, "That's your job."

I suggested, "Let him be with the poop in his pants until we're finished," which is exactly what he did. When we finished the session, I helped her empower herself so she could stand up for herself, which had been her real reason for wanting the session in the first place.

When she confronted her husband for letting their son walk around with poop in his pants for over an hour, he reacted angrily. (Note: the boy was three and not yet potty-trained, something I think he was resisting as a way to get attention from his father.) She handed her husband a diaper and the clean-up supplies, both of which he threw on the floor. I said to him, "Maybe you need to make this a hundred percent relationship and learn how to clean your son up yourself. This is just an indication he wants your attention. He will stop when you begin to recognize him and give him attention. There's no line as to who's responsible for taking care of children's needs."

At this point, he began to use four-letter cuss words at me and his wife about what he was and was not going to do. The child was still in the room and observing his out-of-control father's ranting, and his mother, who was unable to cope and began crying. She eventually opted to change their son's diaper. The bewildered father was angry and lost as to what to do in this crisis. He maintained an illusion of power by getting mad at me for upsetting the balance in his family. The crucial element of this story is: What was this three-year-old boy observing and faithfully recording in his subconscious mind? And how has the fact that his father did not want to care for him scarred him emotionally for the rest of his life? Parents such as this are creating the next generation of clients for practitioners such as myself.

As a footnote, the next time I went to their house to pick up some product, the father would not let me in the house so his wife and I had to conclude our business out on the sidewalk. Needless to say, I no longer do business with him.

Just walk through any department store or supermarket and watch how parents deal with their children. Now, children must learn to balance their need to be autonomous individuals with their need to function within the family group, so the parents' job is to instill children with a set of behavioral boundaries, or rules governing how they work within the family and the larger community. These rules are usually enforced by children's need for approval and acceptance by the group, and failing that, infractions should carry clearly delineated consequences, worked out jointly by parents and children. Most parents confuse discipline with punishment, but a healthy discipline is really guidance as to behavior and reinforcement of that behavior, backed by consistent love, boundaries and clearly stated consequences for errant behavior. Then, if the child breaks the rules, the punishment comes as no surprise, which means there's no blame or anger, and the automatic nature of the consequence leaves the child's self-esteem intact. Spanking on the spot does nothing but erode the child's trust in the parents

In my experience with my own children and those with whom I have worked, there is no need for any kind of punishment if you build trust into your relationship with your child. When they respect you, they will mind you. Most people assume force proves dominance and control, but all it does is make a child shut down or act more belligerently. Respect and trust go down the drain.

The worst kind of punishment is withholding love or threatening survival, because that adds anxiety on top of guilt, and further erodes self-esteem. On the other hand, boundaries tell children they are cared for and safe. If parents start instilling this "code of morality" in a child young enough, they will not have any challenges, but most parents do not train their children, and simply react when confronted with problem behavior. Most children are actually only trying to get attention and recognition, but if you slap their hands or wrestle with them in the store over some item they have picked up, you have a win/lose confrontation, which you will win because ultimately, you have the authority. But in the end, the erosion of the child's respect for you means you always lose and trust is eroded more each time this happens.

Children want attention; you want them to follow directions you make up as you go along. As a result, your needs are not met because the child disobeys you, so you withdraw love, and he or she feels rejected and not understood. Over a period of time, the child begins to feel not only rejected, but also that you do not accept him, which even actually leads to feeling, "I am not all right and I am not loved."

To compensate and mitigate the pain of feeling unloved, the child may go one step further. He may reduce his expectation of love by believing, "I am unworthy of love." Thus, the next time you withdraw your love, the pain is less because he/she begins to not expect your love. However this behavior ruins their chances for fulfilling relationships. This is what happened to us as children, so we just repeat the behavior pattern we learned as a child, rebuilding the destructive patterns of the past.

In the following case, we see a classic example of suppression and denial: A baby born ten years after the last child is a "mistake" and the mother almost dies in childbirth. The three-day-old baby is in bed, nursing on her mother's breast, when the father bursts into the room and lambastes the mother with foul language. "Why the bleep did you decide you needed to have another kid? We can't afford the three we already have and I am having to pay for live-in childcare because you have to stay here another week. What if you'd died? Where would that leave me?"

Now the mother did not want to have the baby in the first place. She would have elected to have an abortion but for her family's religious beliefs. Lying in a hospital bed, weak from loss of blood through hemorrhaging almost to death, she can't defend herself, and puts up with her husband's bad-tempered harangues. However, three-day-old Emily (not her real name) records the entire conversation and its underlying energy of the father condemning her for their financial plight and for almost having killed her mother. From deep in her subconscious mind, this argument rules Emily's behavior for the next 47 years, but consciously she knows nothing of what happened in the hospital that day. She's just very aware today, 47 years later, that her father never liked her because he constantly mistreated her throughout her childhood. The impact on Emily's life had been tragic ... until she came to one of my lectures. When she told me her story, she added, "My life has been a living hell. Living with a father who despised me and told me so every day was traumatic. I avoided him at all costs. I just don't know why he hated me so much. I left home at sixteen by getting married to the first guy who came along, but that didn't work at all. I got pregnant, and stuck in the relationship until I could get a job and support myself and my son. I married four more times, but they never worked out because my husbands treated me the same way my father did. Now I have four children whose lives aren't working either. I've had sixteen jobs, and ended up getting fired each time. I'm not a bad person, but what have I done to deserve this?"

I've shortened Emily's story somewhat, but it shows how we persecute ourselves over simple rejection by another person. The core of the problem was that her young, open mind had recorded a set of programs that held the belief that she had almost caused her mother's death so she had to be punished. Of course, this was totally false, but once the mind sets up programs, it is controlled by them until they are cleared and deleted from the subconscious mind's database. Our mind is strictly literal in its interpretation and tries to solve the problem using its own corrupted, flawed programming. If we do not know what the issue is, how can we resolve it without destroying our children's lives, as she has done.

The real reason Emily's mother almost died was because she had been under verbal and emotional attack throughout her marriage and pregnancy, and no longer wanted to face her husband. At least she did not take the escape hatch, and *did* stay around to learn the lesson the best she could. She had tried to give Emily the best support she could, but the father's vicious onslaughts had resulted in devastating programming *in utero* and during her early years, including every rejection program a person could possibly have.

Emily's choice of husbands reflected her drive to heal the relationship with her father, and to finally get the love from him that she craved. However, those choices brought her only men who were as violent and vindictive as her father had been.

We cleared all of Emily's programming so she could start her new life and function again, by forgiving her mother and father plus all five husbands and releasing all the negative programming. After we did all the damage control and set her on a new life path, she was able to make peace with her children and start a new life. It took a few years to do the damage control with her children. Six months later, Emily called to tell me that, for the first time in her life, she had a supportive job position with a company who really appreciated her ability as a good worker. In six months, the owner of the company was attracted to her, and a new and very different supportive and loving relationship evolved from this. Quite different from the past five men. They had planned a family gathering with her children at Christmas and everything was going perfectly. She eventually married her new friend and he adopted her children.

Children are looking for attention, approval, validation and recognition all the time unless they get it in functional family. A case in point: Mother is hurried to get her two children to school on time and get to work. They are feeling the lack of attention from their mother because she works full time and they have to go to child care after school until she picks them up. Children will get attention no matter how they get it. They do not look at the consequences of their negative behavior because any form of attention will do. The children are slow at getting dressed, then slow at eating breakfast. Mother, agitated and irritated, is pushing them and gets no breakfast. They get in the car because they missed the bus and start throwing things at each other. Mother is trying to drive and control them at the same time. They are late to school and so she blames it on them. She knows she will be late to work and blames that on them, too. Who is at fault here? It is obvious this mother needs reparenting so she can get a handle on her own behavior. It is not the children's problem. They want attention. They do not care how they get it. They were able to get negative attention but did that work for them. How do you think their day went at school? The mother gets a call that her son is disrupting the class and the teacher wants to talk with her. Who is going to find the time to do this? She does not have enough time to provide quality time for them now. Her husband is very little help in the situation. Is this relationship headed for crash on the rocks? When she came to see me, she was beside herself and had major pain in her neck, shoulders and upper back. The medical people did not know what to do. They prescribed psycho-active drugs. The school wanted her to give Ritalin to her son to calm him down. We released all the anger at her mother and the childhood programming to begin with which started her on the right track.

In later sessions, we released the anger at her father and her husband who was the father replacement. She began to see that the children were not the problem. She was the problem. As we went through the reparenting process, her children calmed down as she saw she needed to reparent them so they could recover all the lost time from the past. They are not acting out anymore as they can feel they are accepted and validated. The situation with her husband was not going very smoothly but she was empowered to the point she could stand her own ground and say how she felt. She was now pain free and could handle her situation quite well. How long will this marriage last at this point? I doubt it will survive as she is now empowering herself to stand up and say what she feels. If he will take more responsibility in the relationship, then it will last. The result of this was he came to see me a couple of times and everything smoothed out for six months. Then he fell back into his old behavior and the relationship ended in divorce.

In the course of investigating the cause of my own pain, I took a look at all the clients who came to me; I was having remarkable results with some but not all of the people. At this time, I was practicing conventional talk therapy. The old statement, "When the student is ready the teacher appears," is exactly what happened.

In 1984, I found the answer with a client named Dave, who was having problems working with women who were his supervisors. He had grown up with a domineering and controlling mother who had physically abused him. As a child, he had developed a fear of women so, as an adult, it was natural for him to be afraid of women in power, such as female supervisors. They would treat him well, but he'd just be waiting for something to drop down on him, as it had in childhood. We discovered that he did not know what love was, so he felt that female bosses were setting him up, just as his mother used to do. The further we went into his issues, the more intense the pain that started coming up in his body. Next, we found he had a shell around him so he would not feel emotional pain. When we started breaking up the shell, the pain got progressively worse. After a few sessions, he was wondering if the pain was going to be cleared or get worse. He came to the next session with severe pain around one shoulder blade so I put him on my massage table and tried to locate the pain and its cause. To my surprise, his body began to talk to me, telling me what the conflict was, just as if I was playing a tape recording. At that moment, psychotherapy and I went our different ways. I recognized that childhood information remains locked in cellular memory. My intuitive self told me to create an affirmation about forgiving his mother and himself, and the pain would go away, so I had him repeat the affirmation after me, and the pain was totally released and never came back.

In future sessions, we worked around his body, looking for painful spots. We were able to release all his emotional blocks and get him back on his feet so he could function as a normal person. Relations with his female supervisor smoothed out to the point where she became the caring mother he'd never had. All his relationships with women improved and he was finally able to feel happiness and joy in his life. His final comment to me after our last session was, "I have never felt this good in my life and I'm getting to like my supervisor at work. I have no problems sleeping anymore and the pain I've endured for twenty years is all gone." (Until that breakthrough session, he'd never mentioned any pain because he'd assumed it was a physical issue and not an emotional one.)

After the sessions with Dave, I switched my whole practice over to hands-on therapy. I had finally found the key to releasing both an emotional issue and the associated physical pain at the same time. This was the beginning of a whole new practice. I lost some clients who said they didn't want to participate in my new approach, but I later learned they shied away because the controllers in their mind were bringing up fear in them. They had no control over their lives because they were on autopilot and Conscious Controlling Mind was controlling them, so they reacted without conscious control. I did not find this concept until 15 years later, when I was trying to figure out why clients would not return for sessions when I knew they had much more that had to be released.

I found this out with a client who made an appointment at a lecture I gave at a bookstore. Oddly, she called me twice to confirm the directions to my office and in the session, I discovered why. She was scared and really wanted to have the session but her mind kept telling her not to. On her way to my office, her car engine began to misfire, and finally stopped. An auto mechanic could find nothing wrong with the car so she set out again on her way. Five blocks later, the car stalled so she parked and caught a bus to my office. She said, "I left home an hour and half early because I knew something like this was going to happen." When she calmed down, we discovered that her mind had actually stopped the car in an effort to prevent her from getting to the session. When we broke through the fear, we discovered it dated back to the first day of her life.

Since then, I've had many more instances of this resistance, the most extreme of which was the client's new car that caught fire and burned to the ground. Our mind is an awesomely powerful computer, but why do we let it torpedo our life? Because we do not know this is happening.

I am always amazed by what forgiveness will do to heal ruptured family relationships. It is the only way to perform damage control to heal relationships. Unfortunately very few troubled people find this avenue because they are unable to let go of their anger and resentment.

By proper planning in our lives before even thinking about marriage, we must remove all the negative programming and take all the skeletons out of our closet so they do not start rattling later in our relationships causing breakdowns, burn outs and divorce.

What it comes down to is, are we willing to listen to our children and ask them what their opinion is or what their perception and interpretation is? If we had their trust and they knew we would not react, they would confide in us. The only reason to lie or not tell the truth is fear of reprisal and punishment. When we're able to listen and build our children's confidence and trust, we listen with no reaction, and we be able to solve any conflict or problem without fear.

4

The Path to Recovery

Fortunately, over the last 15 years, a small number of people have been trying to turn back the tide and create functional families. They are becoming aware that to successfully raise children, they must have their own lives in order, which often means "recovery." And *ReParenting*.

To get on the path to recovery, we must set up a plan for our lives. In my practice, I find that few people have any plan for their life and wander through the years without a map, hoping to stumble onto the right path. Or maybe they don't even know there is a path. But, without a plan, even if they did find the right path, they would not even know it *was* the right path. Do you think a manager would run a business in this manner? Highly unlikely.

Such people get into relationships without understanding the source of the attraction. And, statistically, more than 50 percent of marriages end in divorce. (This does not even count the nonfunctional relationships where the partners are coexisting basically as strangers living in the same house.)

Most people go into relationships looking for security, safety, and common interests. Most codependent people are looking for someone to validate and love them. Further, many people confuse sex and love so, if they have exhilarating early sexual experiences, they mistake good body chemistry for love and decide that this is the "right" person with whom to partner in life. (I have worked with many people who feel the only time they are receiving love is during sexual encounters so they become addicted to sex.) Just as good parenting begins with being good parents, *finding* the right person as a life mate begins with *being* the right person yourself.

However, less than five percent of those looking for romantic relationships make an effort to get their own life in order so that they can recognize and attract a partner with whom they can create a functional relationship. Most people are looking for love in the wrong places.

Almost all people jump into relationships not knowing why or what about the other person attracts them. Even though I had studied how to create a successful relationship, getting past the pitfalls on the path still took my wife and I 15 years. In our path to finding the way, we came close to divorcing at least three times. One of them was a serious breach of confidence, yet we stayed the course, knowing that our two children needed functional parents. We also knew that we had ended up in this relationship to learn the lessons that were before us at the time, and that if we had run away from those lessons, we would simply have needed to tackle them with another person after starting over. So we decided to work through the lessons that were slapping us in the face.

Before a relationship goes too far and is locked in with children, a couple should at least try to learn why they are in that relationship. They must *ReParent* themselves and grow to become aware, functional adults before they even think about bringing the next generation into the world. Most people do not even have the first basic understanding of what a functional relationship is before they jump in.

For the majority of people looking for a relationship, it is like firing a shotgun, with pellets spraying everywhere but with no focus. We hit on someone and then begin to get them to like us. There are many reasons for attraction, and we must understand that there is more to relationships than the purely physical level. The following reasons for attraction are ranked from the most to the least common:

1. Substituting or replacing your parents, so that you can heal your relationship with them through your partner. It makes no difference if it is a hetero or gay relationship.
2. Discharging past life karma with your mate.
3. Relationship addiction.
4. Reliving mother/son or father/daughter relationships.
5. The deceptive persona, i.e., one partner is fooled by the mask worn by the other until the true self opens up and you see who the person really is.
6. Relationship of convenience, which is little more than two roommates living together.
7. Sex addiction.

8. Common interests, i.e., a platonic friendship under the same roof.

9. Arranged marriage.

10. Unconditionally loving, functional relationship.

Nobody "falls" in love; it just does not happen. In fact, they come under one of the first eight categories. Many people want to believe they fall into the last category, but I can count on two hands such couples I've met over the last 30 years. I have found we *can* create a #10 type relationship after the parties in the relationship have cleared all the lessons that cause problems.

Few *successful* relationships begin with a love attraction, mainly because less than ten percent of the population has the slightest idea what love is. In practice, the number of people who can actually function with unconditional love is probably less than two percent, but creating a functional family requires both parties to be capable of a type 10 relationship.

When I was in my 20s and 30s, I would not even use the word "love" because it scared me. I knew I didn't know what love was about because I'd never received any as a child. When Susie would ask me, "Do you love me?" I would automatically reply, "You know I do."

After attending a workshop that turned my life around in 1978, I was able to say, "I love you" to her and know what that meant. My experience with clients has revealed that most people do not know what love is, nor do they know how to give and receive love. So how can parents impart a love model to their children when they don't even know themselves what love is? Children learn by example, by watching what their parents do, not by listening to what they say. So if they do not see their parents acting lovingly to each other, how can the children grow up with a love model in their lives?

In 1978, actually feeling what love is was a new experience for me. What most people describe as love is really "conditional acceptance," or attention-bartering, complete with hooks and strings as in, "If you do it my way, or accept what I say, or stroke my fears away, then I will tell you I love you."

When Susie and I were married, she initially saw me as a mother substitute, and I acted out the exact personality traits she had not worked out with her mother. (We will be attracted to a person who will satisfy or meet our need to complete our life plan.) My reality was very fragile, and I was committed to being in control so as to avoid the same mistakes my friends were making. This allowed me to feel safe and secure, but led me into being a counter-dependent. I vowed to be dependent on no one, but I also depended on people who would let me control them when they were around me.

So Susie and I entered our relationship not knowing we were playing out our needs in ways we knew nothing about. We also had many karmic past life lessons listed in our flight plans, too. Ten years passed before we became aware of the roles we were playing in our life drama, and could begin to correct our behavior patterns. We knew we were on an unstable footing yet were unable to make much headway. Three years later, when I attended a seminar on how to recognize and avoid the pitfalls of relationships, we made a major leap forward in our ability to communicate and understand ourselves.

We discovered that our parents' behavior was still sneaking into ours. At the seminar, we discovered that incarnating souls choose the parents they will need for the lessons they seek to learn in that life. If the lessons do not work out, the person will find a partner, employer or some other person who fits that need. Who the other players are or what their gender is is less important than the personality traits needed for the lesson. We are committed to the lesson and will pursue it until we work through it.

Seldom do we know, however, why we are attracted to that specific person. We followed the "marriage plan" that we'd set up so we could avoid challenges yet, after four years, we found we still had a missing ingredient – "unconditional love." Getting love to work for us took nine more years, but once we did, we traded roles. Susie went back to work and I stayed home with our two young boys, and quickly learned a lot about the every-day running of a household. Because of the cultural prejudice about gender roles, you cannot really have a 100 percent relationship unless you can shift roles. When you have children, there can be no division as who has to assume what responsibility. You must deal with the challenges as they come up.

How can parents hope to bring children into this world who will grow up into a functional adults if the parents do not know who they are themselves? And if they are laboring under the stress of lessons, how can they even function and provide their children with a foundation for a supportive lifestyle or a blueprint for the child's healthy adulthood? As Susie and I discovered, creating a functional family takes much preparation.

From the above list, most relationship attraction is parental replacement and past-life karma. When a karmic lesson comes up, people are attracted to the lesson and the person with whom to learn it. Therefore, I encourage people who are starting a new relationship to see me so that we can unwind any past-life lessons that can cause relationship addiction. Many times, people starting a new relationship that is "firecrackers" are actually being attracted to an unresolved past-life lesson. If both partners will work with me, clearing the lessons can put the relationship on a more solid footing, which may be the beginning of a functional family. If only one party is willing, then the relationship usually dissolves. If it doesn't, they are heading for a dysfunctional family and problems that will cause the relationship to fall apart in future years.

Relationship addiction can have many "hooks" that draw a person into a relationship. Many people will get fired up with, "This is it! This is my soul mate! I just know it!" Then, when reality sets in, they find they cannot function in the relationship until they understand the nature of the lessons. Some people will exit via divorce; others will seek marriage counseling.

In my therapy practice, I soon realized that I could not help clients who could only blame their partners and not do the inner work on themselves. How could I work to resolve the problems in the relationship when the clients did not understand themselves or the challenges they were facing?

Many people ask me to describe the workshop I attended that turned my life around. It was a very confrontational workshop which was series of seminars on finding out who you are. Paul would describe the process in a lecture and then we would work in groups of four working on the process. You had to be willing to allow other participants to ask any questions to get to your resistances and break them down. This was the introductory seminar, and lasted four days.

At one of the workshops, I blacked out for three hours during the lecture. It took one of the trainers almost three hours to get to the bottom of my fear which caused me to black out. We had upset my whole basic operating program for my life. At this seminar, which was a two-week live-in series of workshops, we started with 47 people and 11 people left before the two weeks were finished. It was an expensive seminar which included rooms and all our meals yet people filtered out when they could not handle the content, but if you left there were no refunds.

5

Understanding Relationship Types

Mother/Son, Father/Daughter Relationships

These are codependent relationships. Men who had strong, ma-
nipulative, controlling mothers will gravitate to women with
the same character traits. Many of these women would much
rather have a supportive relationship but they find themselves
not only being mothers to the children, but to their husbands,
too. Most often, the mother/son relationships fail as the husband cannot fulfill the father role. If the relationship does hold
together, it has damaging effects on the children because they
see a father who is weak and can't give them what they want
from him – a strong male role model/example.

Father/Daughter relationships are far more prevalent than
one would expect. Many women are from families with weak

mothers and controlling fathers, which sets women up for this type of relationship. Tied into parental substitution and past life karmic lessons, the strong man/weak woman role models can be detrimental to children. This behavior pattern was passed down from family to family as the man was seen as the provider and all-powerful head of the family. In history, women have always deferred to men, which sets up a codependent pattern. This pattern works well for men who play the macho "strong guy," and may be avidly copied by the male children. Hopefully, female children will react against the mother's weakness and resolve to not copy it. With the women's liberation movement, this relationship pattern is dying out but still remains one of the most common dysfunctional relationships. Most of these are adult children emotionally stuck in childhood, usually between ten and fourteen years old. It is curious to note that over 50% of the relationships today are of this form of relationship.

The Deceptive Person

Many times, a person will put up an illusionary front and heap lavish praise on the other party. However, this deceptive persona is pure bait. If we take the bait without using our discernment, we will eventually discover the truth, hopefully before we make a commitment. Quite often, the deception continues for some time, but the facade will crack eventually, and the sudden on-rush of reality can be a shock to the deceived party. Often the deceiver gets away with it because of exceptional beauty or good looks, and benefits from the "halo effect" in which one outstanding attribute (the halo) overwhelms several less desirable qualities. When the other party sees through this, the relationship crashes. Most deceivers are men, and potential partners must know why they are going into the relationship before they can create a functional relationship.

Relationships of Convenience

These may work sometimes, but usually on a codependent basis. They usually involve "adult children" and what happens depends on who grows up first or if they both wake up together. Quite often, the relationship can have father/daughter or mother/son elements, too. Usually the partners do not want to make any decisions so they accept the first person who feels comfortable and does not confront any of their fears or insecurity. This often occurs with teenagers who marry to get away from their parents. It can work if both partners remain satisfied with a superficial, noncommittal relationship.

Sex Addiction

This program comes from childhood interpretation of a serious rejection issue and, as adults, they feel the closeness of sex provides them with love. As a result, they only feel love during sexual encounters. This can destroy a relationship very quickly, depending on which partner is addicted. If it's the woman, most men will accept her excess sexual desire, so it's less of a problem than when the man is addicted. In those cases, women may feel that the man's need and aggression makes them a sex object. This will cause men to feel rejected, and may result in them looking outside the relationship to have their overwhelming needs met, even though they know it may end the relationship. I see many upset female clients who have a lower sex drive than her partner; seldom do I see men. One of my clients gave her husband a second chance if he would see me. In the session, he admitted this was his third extramarital affair. Six months later, it happened again, so he returned. Typical of many men I see, he had strong feelings of rejection by his mother and other women in his life. Before they have any children, sex addicts must release the addiction totally.

Common Interest Relationships

These will work unless other complications cloud up the issue. They usually start out well but degrade as other issues begin to arise ... which they always seem to do. We cannot keep a relationship going with only a shared interest to hold it together. Sometimes these types of relationships are covers for more serious emotional dysfunction that is covered up in denial. Sometimes the common interest will be an addiction, which means that the partners are not suitable parents.

Arranged Marriages

This type of relationship has just about disappeared, thanks to the self-interest and willpower of today's young people. However, they can work if the partners have some common interests and can develop an accepting, loving relationship. I have worked with a few but most of them fall apart when one or both partners gain some control over their lives. A good example of this was a woman who was referred to me by a friend. She was a debutante from a wealthy family who went to all the right schools, universities, functions and presented the proper facade that her parents demanded of her.

In a session, she confided, "When I was walking down the aisle at my wedding with my father, I just wanted to run away. I did not want to get married then or to the man I was about to wed. But I didn't want to embarrass my family because this was a big occasion for them, so I went along with it. My fiancé was in medical school and our first child came along before he graduated, which complicated the relationship. My guilt kept me in the relationship for the child's sake. When the second child came along, I felt totally trapped and suffered through it for twenty years for the children's sake."

Her inner suppressed anger and feelings of futility affected the children in a major way. She brought the two sons to see me but I got nowhere with them because of their resentment towards their father, who was never there for them. And, even though it was covered up, her anger had an effect on them, too. When we released all the anger and guilt, the mother decided she needed to reclaim her life so she gave the children, now 16 and 18, a choice; they could stay with their father or leave with her. They elected to stay with their father because he had the money to buy them off with material rewards. The older son went to college five months later, which caused major adjustment difficulties for the younger boy. He had problems in school after the separation because the father did not change his behavior, so now the younger boy was alone, without his older brother to be there for him as a stabilizing influence. After the divorce, the mother said, "I feel free for the first time in my life." Of course, her parents had a fit because they were affected by the stigma of their daughter's "failed marriage." When she was finally able to talk with them about all the feelings she had suppressed for over 20 years, they refused to own their behavior and their needs, which had caused her to acquiesce to their demands. However, she did not let that stop her from clearing her feelings and walking away, clear of guilt for the first time in her life. She had a harder time dealing with her children due their resentment and feelings of abandonment, but she was no longer buying into the guilt trips.

The biggest problems we have in life stem from selling out to our need for validation and acceptance. We fall into this trap primarily because we are so afraid of rejection that we tell people what they want to hear, in exchange for their acceptance.

Over the years, I drilled into my children to not allow other people to manipulate you into taking their bait. Look out for number one first, of course, without being rude or discourteous. The only person who can hurt you is you. Nobody can hurt you unless you let them.

Unconditionally Loving Functional Relationships

As said earlier, I have met fewer than ten couples who have this relationship working in their life. It is rare because most people cannot balance being independent yet interdependent. But, only if we can do this can we teach it to our children. Children learn by example, so we must model this behavior for them. If we ask people, "Can you love yourself and receive love?" they will say yes but it's rare to find people who can be honest with themselves about their relationship with themselves.

Mastery of this type of relationship is the goal of this book and will be discussed throughout its pages, with a summation in the final chapter of the qualities of this relationship in relation to ourselves and our children.

The original recovery movement started many years ago with Alcoholics Anonymous and, over the last 20 years, many people have said to themselves, "I feel the same way they feel but alcohol is not my addiction," so they formed groups to talk about their feelings and experiences. This blossomed into the "recovery industry," based on the AA model. Some of my friends who have been divorced and would not listen to me about why their relationships failed in the past are now members of Codependents Anonymous, Adult Children of Alcoholics, etc. At least they are recognizing their challenges and doing something about it before they make any more mistakes. Unfortunately, it is too late for their grown children, but the parents are aware now and making peace with their children, to develop loving relationships that break the pattern of inheriting and passing on problem beliefs and behaviors so their grandchildren do not have to grow up with negative programming. The path to recovery is out there; all we need do is find it. We are all entitled to unconditional love, peace, happiness, harmony, joy, acceptance, approval, validation, acknowledgment, and recognition.

In Summary

1. If you are attracted by relationship addiction, sex attraction or parental substitution, etc., it would be best to get an evaluation from a qualified therapist who can help clear all the programs that would cause you to draw in a dysfunctional partner to learn the lessons. Our mind has a radar set-up that will evaluate potential partners for you and set up a smoke screen so you will not know why you are being attracted to various people. Even though you recognize the situation, you will continue to draw the inappropriate person into your life. Your mind will not allow you to attract a functional person to you. They will avoid you based on the metacommunication you send out to potential partners. This is why people end up in a string of relationships that do not work.

2. Until you clear the program that draws these lessons to you, your radar will pick the partner out for you. You have no choice in the matter. You will feel you are making the right decision but the skeletons in your closet will eventually start shaking and the relationship will begin to crumble.

3. I have had many people come to see me with a list of qualities they want in a potential partner. They know exactly what they want, yet they cannot find the person who matches their want list. Many people have come to see me after they made a poor choice and are locked in with children they know are not being treated right, yet they cannot change the pattern. This is the mistake of not evaluating their readiness for a relationship and all the potential blocks that might be in the path.

4. You can't find love if you are looking in the wrong places and do not know what it is to begin with. I will repeat this over

and over in this book. Unconditional love and forgiveness are the keys to a successful relationship and raising children with self-esteem, self-worth and self-confidence. There is no other formula that works without these qualities. Children learn by demonstrating examples and they follow your lead in every aspect of their lives.

Here is an example of picking the wrong person. I was asked where were you when I needed you. I told her she probably would not have recognized she needed my help when she was getting married because she was in an illusion thinking she was making the right choice.

Sixteen years and two children later, she recognized her relationship could not be saved. After a year of working with me, she finally faced up to the fact she was heading to a divorce which she did finalize. The interesting note in this is even though she knew why she had to get out of the relationship and had assumed she learned the lesson it was still coming up. She went through three online computer relationship matchups drawing into her the same type of person she divorced. A 12-year-old boy. It was very frustrating because they would have all the right qualifications until she spent time with them, which revealed they were little boys.

After over two years of trying to find the lesson, we finally found it. Her mother had warned her about these predatory men who will take advantage of you. Mother's statement to her young daughter was; "You must find a nice man who will take care of you so you can have good children and live happy all your life." What interpretation does her young mind make out of this? This type of man cannot be aggressive or assertive. He must be a nice supportive man. Since her parenting model is a controlling woman who used a control, authority, discipline and compliance model and her father is a wimp who she pushes around, who do you think she is going to choose? A young boy who is an adult child..

Since her mind still has this program installed in her mind she continues to draw these type of men to her. This is very frustrating to her. When we discovered the program and released it, new men who were the type she was looking for began to appear in her life. Now she has a functional relationship with a man who fits her needs and desires.

Where does this leave us and how do we get to the Promised Land? As I stated earlier, we have to be able to recognize we have a conflict. Once we get out of the illusion and face the fact that we have to make changes in our lives, we can begin the shift to re-write the scripts we have been following until we recognized our lives were not working.

The main problem we have is to recognize and accept that the path we have been taking did not work.

Then we have to decide how we are going to get off the detour and take the path to success in our lives. We have to decide if we are willing to face all the garbage we created in childhood by following our parents' patterns. Whose life are you living – your parents or yours? When you make a decision to get on with your life, you have made the first decision.

You could allow yourself to believe that changing your path can be hard and difficult, which will create all kinds of crisis situations you will have to handle. Are you going to suffer and struggle to obtain your goal? You do not have to take the difficult road to reach your goal. It does not have to be this way unless you want to believe this false concept. You are the only one who can place limitations on yourself. It is this way: Do you want to believe that the big lie you have been led to believe that life is tough and you have to work hard and live in pain? Or do you want to take the easy path to success and except the challenge?

The challenge is before you. That is why you're reading this book. You can meet the challenge head on and change your life now. Are you ready for peace, happiness, harmony, joy and unconditional acceptance and love?

Are you going to give yourself permission to go for it, or are you going to follow the path you're on which does not work for you? It really is that simple. Are you willing to let go and release all the negative feelings, shadow memories and re-pressed beliefs about what love has been for you from your childhood? For most people, love was indifference. Nobody really cared. Most people do not even recognize this is how they feel about love. In fact most people think they know what love is so they use the word in many conversations with reckless abandon.

We have developed a system where you can begin the *ReParenting* process on your own.

It is much faster to work with one of our therapists but can work with the home study course to Reparenting Yourself. It is a home study manual using affirmations I call "dialogues with your mind." There are a lot of self-examination exercises in the course to find out what you think of yourself and what you need to change. It will be available in August 2009.

6

The Perfect Relationship

Most people view relationships as being outside of self. The problem with this is that all relationships begin with *ourselves, not with others*. We must develop an effective relationship with self before we can extend out to connecting with others. We had a good relationship with self when we were born.

In 24,999 out of 25,000 births, the relationship with self was compromised before or after birth. The major conflict started with the mother. (We are not blaming her, for she did the best she could working under her dysfunctional relationship with herself. She just happened to be the person you identified with as your primary caregiver after you were born.)

If your parents had an effective relationship with themselves and each other, then there is a possibility they could have helped you build an effective relationship with yourself. If you were the exception who had parents from a functional family or who recognized the mistakes your parents made, then you may have the opportunity to grow up in a functional family. If your parents recognized the conflicts that caused them to be imprinted with negative behavior or you have chosen to stop the vicious cycle, then you may understand the process of *ReParenting*. If your parents were able to recognize this vicious cycle of handing off their parents' dysfunctional relationship to their children, you were fortunate to have parents with vision and awareness. As you can see from the examples in this book, it does not guarantee you will have successful relationships unless you have cleared all the skeletons in your closet.

Adopted children have much more complex issues, even if they had a totally functional relationship with their adopted parents, as you also can see from the examples in this book. Adopted children have deeply seated rejection issues that must be cleared up with their birth parents, or they will cause many rejection issues in their relationships in turn. Most of the time, these issues are buried in denial files so they do not have to deal with the pain of feeling lost, rejected and abandoned. These issues must be cleared for an effective life as an adult.

As I said earlier, functional relationships do not happen very often. More than likely your mother did not have an effective relationship with herself or her husband. As a result, unfortunately, your relationship with self began to break down shortly after birth. She probably was not able to bond with you at birth either. Up to 95% of the time, you had a traumatic birth experience because the doctors either did not want to recognize birth without violence or they were ignorant that there was a better, more loving way to bring a baby into this world.

So where are we in finding the right path in this jungle of dysfunctional behavior patterns? As described earlier, mother did not know what love was, so how could she demonstrate this to you? Along with all the other rejection feelings you may have had, plus feeling your mother was deliberately withholding love from you, your relationship with self began to break down. It deteriorated into self-rejection, feeling non-acceptance rather than self-acceptance. The more you tried to get love and recognition from mother, the more you felt rejected because she first became irritated, then became angry, because she could not control your behavior. As a result, you became angry at her for not meeting your need for love and recognition. When you realized that to push for love was getting you nowhere except more rejection, you began to give up the need, and backed down in most cases. And by the time you were four, you'd finally given up completely. So, by four years of age, you'd decided your mother was right, and that you were unlovable. At that point, any form of attention, even violence, was interpreted as love because you simply wanted recognition in some form. And the tragic bottom line was that you were left not knowing what love was, something that still haunts you today in your search for fulfilling relationships.

There are those children who are labeled reactionary who do not give up. What we do with them is pump them up with drugs to slow and calm them down, but drugs such as Ritalin just complicate the situation, not solve it. We must ask, "Why is the child acting out?" Nowadays, they are labeled "Radical Associative Disorder" (RAD) children. (More on this in Volume Two.)

As a result, RAD children grew up thinking attention in any form was love. As a result, when they want something, they think acting out and reacting will get them what they want. Many times it does because the parents cannot deal with the reactive behavior any longer so they give in. Not knowing there are better ways to handle this the behavior pattern, they give up because they only know the control, authority, discipline and compliance parenting model. It definitely does not work with reactionary children because this is what causes their behavior. If parents could get their respect so they could trust their parents, knowing they could get recognition and acceptance, we would see a major shift in their behavior pattern. The only challenge is we must work with the parent first so they can install the qualities of unconditional love in their mind first. Then the child will recognize this and respond in a more effective manner

Attention, love and recognition are very important to young people. Hearing all the different definitions of love in the movies, on TV and music, they began to accept love was external so they used their bodies to get love and acceptance and recognition. This is one fact many people do not want to face. With all the media attention on sex and the social networking sites on the internet sex is out there. Did you ever wonder why so many young girls get in trouble with sex? Many times they accepted sexual relationships as being love, and became misdirected, thinking they had to have attractive bodies to be acceptable and get recognition. Many are asking for plastic surgery to increase the size of their breasts as young as age fourteen. And we find many have bulimia and anorexia eating disorders. Others who cannot reduce their weight go into self-rejection and depression.

Many RAD boys grow into men who will not even try to approach relationships, so live a solitary life or become workaholics. This could be cleared up by simply releasing the fear of commitment and fear intimacy. This way we can build up their self-esteem, self-worth and self-confidence. It is a sad story when you realize most people are functioning under false beliefs.

Quite a few people ask me how do you reparent yourself? I touch on this all my lectures plus we are writing a home study course on reparenting. This book is full of examples of reparenting, yet I find people who do not seem to understand that reparenting is very simple process.

Let's review a little about relationships. To develop perfect relationships, we start with self. We can assume that we cannot develop effective relationships with others, including children, until we recover our lost selves and have healed the separation with self. When statistics indicate that less than 20% of those in developed nations have a reasonable relationship with self, we have a major problem. More than 50% of the population of developed nations are divorced or single. I am not saying you must be in a relationship in any way. Many single people are happy and enjoy their solitude. What I am saying is, we must evaluate our relationship with self based on the peace, happiness, harmony, joy, unconditional love and acceptance we have in our own relationship with self. It has nothing to do with any other person. You have to deal with you first. How others relate to you may be indicators to tell you how you are functioning. The major conflict we have is that it is hard to relate with others to get a handle on how you are appearing to them. The main conflict is everybody wants to see themselves as a supportive person. This is hard to deal with when over 65% of the population operates from fear and 80% operate from behind illusions. Where does this leave us?

Very few people can be objective enough to evaluate themselves to obtain an accurate answer to this question. When I use psychological profile evaluations in question form, we find that less than 65% of the people are answering the questions honestly and accurately. (This sample is skewed because these are only people who already opened up to accepting they need help.) In these profiles, the questions are set up so that you have to answer questions so they line up properly. In other words what it means is all the questions are set up to interlock. If you answer this question in this way there are other questions which must be answered in the same manner to create a pattern. If you do not follow the pattern it will show up as not fitting together. The profile is like a crossword puzzle all pieces have to fit properly or the puzzle will not fit together.

They are set up with questions where you would not do *any* of the four options, yet you have to choose which one you would be least likely to be objectionable to you. Others are set up so you have to choose the option would like to do most, when you would actually like to participate in all of them. They are scored so that each question has a corresponding question it will line up with. Based on this, we can find out how well you are getting along with yourself and others. At least 35% are thrown out because there is no correlation in answers, so they have no value. This means that

65% of the people were honest in their answers, yet less than 10% scored as acceptable in their views of their relationships. Where does this leave us? Is there a way out of this mess? Where do we go from here? If you look at statistics, it does not look as if we have found an effective way out when we have so many dysfunctional relationships today. All you have to do is watch the TV news or read the papers. However, there is hope. There are ways out of this quagmire if you are willing to face the issues and release them. It takes some time and commitment to face the issues. Many people want to bury them and hope they will go away. Unfortunately the issues will rise and start shaking the skeletons your closet and set off disruptive patterns in your life. They will begin setting off disruptive patterns which may create time bombs in your life. They may go off when you least likely expect them in some of the most awkward situations.

How many people are willing to even accept that they *may* need some help? Over the last 30 years in many places where I meet the average person, such as health clubs, churches, seminars, lectures, and workshops, I have held conversations to sample people's attitudes and beliefs. I find what I call the 80-20 rule. Out of 100 people I talk to, 20 percent may be open to discuss this issue. Out of those 20, I again find the 80-20 rule. So the numbers really drop down to 4 percent. So where are we in changing people's beliefs about themselves?

How Do We Develop a Perfect Relationship with Self?

First we must evaluate ourselves to decide whether we even *want* to go down this path. It could be very bumpy, with many boulders in the path you have to navigate around just to stay on the path. You could make it easy for yourself by just confronting the issues and releasing them. Which do you choose? Are you ready to face the music and change the tune in your life? I have found that more than 70% of the people I have talked with are not willing to face their issues. They would rather endure the pain and suffering rather than face the issues. Their beliefs are so strong, they are willing to hold on to them rather than question if they are right. Fear is holding them in a stranglehold which blocks them from facing the issues so they can clear them up.

I have posted on a breast cancer website that claims they are supporting peoples' right to choice in treatment yet I do not get any responses from the people running the website. All I received was complaints and criticism from the people who are members of the social network. Needless to say I have unsubscribed and dropped their website. The same thing happened on the Fibromyalgia social network websites. It is obvious these people are at a dead end in their life but they do not want to hear anything about a positive way out of their dilemma. They are coming from fear of change.

Fear is: *F*alse *E*vidence *A*ppearing *R*eal. Since most of the fear is unreal, how can we even confront it? It takes considerable willpower, commitment and discipline to do so.

If we can, we must look at the first item on the agenda – finding out what real unconditional love is. Then we have to collect all the qualities that surround unconditional love. There are seven qualities surrounding unconditional love. These are qualities our parents could have provided for us with if they had an effective model they could have demonstrated to us and given us.

These are unconditional, with no strings attached, no limiting factors or conditions put on them:

1. Acceptance
2. Recognition
3. Validation
4. Acknowledgment
5. Trust
6. Approval
7. Respect.
8. Unconditional love

These are the qualities of unconditional love. To have an effective relationship with self, we must have these qualities within our own mind so we can demonstrate them to others and our children. Three more cluster qualities can also be separated: Self-Esteem, Self-Worth and Self-Confidence. They are "cluster qualities" in that you cannot have one without the others. The odd situation about these three is that we *do* have them in our Subconscious Mind's database, but they have been overwritten by dysfunctional programs such as, "I'm not all right," "I do not fit in," "I am not accepted," and "Nobody recognizes my abilities."

We must go into the files and locate all these programs and beliefs seeded during childhood and delete the files so we can write new scripts instead. This can be a very easy process or a very long and complicated ordeal. It all depends on your willingness to let go of your past. All it takes is the ability to forgive and accept your caregivers who wrote the faulty programs in your database, usually without knowing what they were doing.

Unfortunately, most books written on how to raise a child are totally off base in their conclusions. Even many of the books in current circulation are providing misdirection on dealing with children's behavior. The majority of them are still advocating the dysfunctional control, authority, manipulation, discipline and compliance model. Even Dr. Spock finally admitted his first books were not good direction, but that was all he knew at the time.

Relationships with self must be to the point where you can accept the seven qualities of love and make them work for you, which means you must allow *you* to validate *you*. Most people are looking for and trying to get outside validation to make themselves feel all right about themselves on the basis that: "If others see me as all right, then I must be all right." One of the outward signs of this is taking over and commandeering a conversation or talking over others by raising your voice to stop them from speaking. Our mind will do this if we do not feel all right about ourselves. Then it will make the assumption that if people allow me to do this, then I am being acknowledged and accepted. A good example of this was a friend of mine who wanted to be accepted so intensely he would actually get rejected, and would do this all the time. He did not even recognize he was doing it. In one instance, I watched the situation and did not say anything, as seven people finally left our one-sided discussion. When we were the only two left, I asked him some questions.

"Do you recognize why everybody else in the group left?" He was so caught up in himself that he didn't even know they'd left. On discussing with him why he did this, he became defensive and angry with me, and told me I was criticizing him. When I asked him, "Why are you refusing to accept the truth?" he walked away.

Eric Fromm, a writer from the 1950s and 1960s, wrote a book when I was in college titled: *The Art of Loving.* This pioneering work on understanding the qualities I am discussing here never really hit the bestseller lists because it offered so many controversial and evolutionary concepts. At the time, I wrote a term paper on the book because I really wanted to learn about what he was promoting. But really understanding the full concept of Fromm's book took me another 15 years. He was so right on that it was amazing but very few people were able accept his concepts. His book would have hit the best seller lists fifty years later because people are finally willing to look at what is missing in their life.

In the 1950s, everybody was recovering from WWII and most situations were not confrontational. There were very few problems. The Korean War was over, we had peace for the first time in twenty years. There was no inflation, people could live comfortably, and suburbia was booming. We were a productive economy, so people made enough money to live comfortably. Even though there were some problems they seemed to be pushed under the table.

One of the big problems was teenage pregnancy. The high school near where I was attending college had 19 girls in the senior class who were pregnant. What these issues indicated was something wrong at home, but we just pulled them out of school and sent them to a home for unwed mothers where they could live and continue their school work. Many of them put their babies up for adoption and some ended up in marriages which did not work out. They blamed it on not having proper education on the subject, so the schools took over the parents' job, but it did not slow down the problem as it did not address the problem directly.

As we progressed, we had to deal with a new issue – young people beginning to think for themselves which was brought on by the hippie generation. The baby boomers' children were breaking away from the happy-go-lucky 1950s and confronting their newfound freedom to break out of the control, authority, manipulation, discipline and compliance parenting program. But unfortunately, they did not create a new pattern. They were fighting the old pattern by just breaking away. I am not going to go through all the history of the movement and the results it created. In short, what has happened is we have never addressed the main problem of children being brought up without knowing what love is. So the pattern which the hippie generation broke away from really did not get addressed and just continues on in another pattern. Why do we have all the problems with gangs, drugs and alcohol? Young people are looking for two things: they are running away from themselves because they do not understand why they feel alone, rejected, not accepted and not alright. What do they do? Run away from themselves with drugs and alcohol or join gangs to create community so they can get validated and accepted by their peer group.

Why is the suicide rate escalating in people under thirty? They are lost and do not know how find their way back to reality from the jungle of feeling not accepted. Where did this start? In Childhood. It will continue to get worse until we confront the challenge; do we correct this vicious circle of passing the dysfunctional parenting pattern on and recycling it generation after generation? It began over two thousand years ago. How are we going to stop it?

One of the major problems we have in communication is incongruent messages. If we are working from a place of not feeling good about ourselves, we will project this message out in what I call "meta-communication." It is a thought-based communication our mind sends out that is nonverbal. Most people don't realize they are picking up the message, yet they will act on it without knowing why they are doing what they do. So it behooves us to clear the incongruent messages our mind is sending out ... and deleting all the files may take some work.

To begin with we must take control over our mind. To do this, we have a protocol with affirmations, or dialogues with our mind to get it working *with* us rather than against us. Going through these dialogues with your mind takes about an hour. We have discovered that some people have conflicts within their mind from trauma as a child, which will try to stop us from reclaiming control. If you have been operating on Autopilot for most of your life, Conscious Controlling Mind, or the autopilot operating system, will resist letting go of control. We can take control back by using the affirmations and once we do, we can reclaim control and begin to clear the cellular Memory.

To get to these programs, we must go through our mind's files like peeling an onion. Each layer will reveal another layer below it. When we peel most of them off, then we begin to take control of our life. As we move into more control, we can empower ourselves to work from a point of power rather than fear.

Once we have understood and can apply the concepts of the qualities of love to ourselves, then we begin by applying them in our relationships with other people. It is almost amazing how people will respond to us when we have a congruent message coming from our own mind.

As we remove all the behavior patterns causing us to act out in the need for control, we find we do not need control any longer, since nobody is threatening us any longer. It was all a *perceived* threat, and not a *real* threat. We find we can cooperate with others with no need to be in control. As we move into this new space of comfort, we find we begin to release stress. There really is no such thing as stress, but only stressed out people. When you no longer react to the stress, it does not affect you.

As you move from a place of neediness, you begin to demand that people treat you in a different way. It is not that you become pushy or outwardly demanding of respect, but you just begin to avoid people who are not operating in your reality. It is almost as if you view the situation and, if it does not meet your needs, you drop it and move on with, "Next!" There is no need to make an issue out of it. If the shoe does not fit, discard it. You are now becoming more comfortable in your life, and it fits better, with no awkwardness. You have a lot more energy because you are not fighting with yourself to play a role.

At this point, you begin to recognize that most people play roles in their life to meet their needs. Some of the major role pairs people play are: "Father/Daughter" and "Mother/Son." As you recover your lost self and grow up again, you can see how you fell into that role. Partnerships in these roles fall apart as soon as one partner begins to see they no longer want to play that role. If both partners can grow up, that's great but it usually does not happen. In most cases, partners break up without ever finding out why the partnership did not work. They go out looking for a new partner, yet they find the same person in a different body and a different name, but with the same behavior patterns. Since they did not explore why the first relationship did not work, they end up in another ill-fated partnership again, which will fall apart due to not evaluating the situation that caused the breakup in the beginning.

In *ReParenting* ourselves, we discover all the imprinted programs we received from our parents or other imprinters that set up the roles we play today. So we get to the point of asking ourselves: "Whose life am I living. A replay of my parents or the life I choose to live?" Usually we find it is *not* the life we thought we were living. So where do we go from here?

With the help of a coach or a therapist, you *can* make major strides. Very few people can make it over the grade without a mentor to help them, preferably one who has the experience of having gone through some of the same experiences you have had. There is a Native-American saying: "You cannot understand my life unless you have walked for a month in my moccasins."

Everybody has different experiences, yet they are all similar in nature. Our mind is a very complex computer, and will make decisions for us until we take control back. Most of the time the decisions are not what we would do if we had control, which is why I say most people have similar repeat experiences because everyone has the same mindset that makes the same decisions until we get control of it.

Now we have grown up, we can take our power back and start on the path to a new life. The choice is yours! Are you ready for peace, happiness, harmony, joy, unconditional love and abundance in your life? There are a lot of bridges to cross and many boulders to push out of the path, yet I know you can do if you apply yourself to the task.

7

Are You Ready to Reparent Yourself? What Does It Require You to Do?

In the response to the review copies of this book, some of the comments I received were, "What is ReParenting? There are no really definitive steps in the book." That surprised me as I thought I put in many examples and had laid it out quite well.

This meant either people were not understanding what I had written or I did not make it clear enough. After talking with many people, I came up with this: If we are confronting behavior patterns but you do not want to see the mistakes, breakdowns and missing aspects of your life, you will not even comprehend what you are reading. Your mind will allow you to pass over anything that confronts you which you do not want to face or address in your life.

If people are in illusion and living totally in the box of that illusion, there is no way they are going to communicate with you about the missing pieces in their life. Maybe they want to believe they have done a good job raising their children or the relationship they are in works even though it is not what they want they want.

If you are a good observer, all you have to do is evaluate the obvious factors that are visible to be able to understand what is not right or missing. The person in the illusion cannot even see the obvious because they must be right to protect themselves. They will defend their position because they are operating out of a defective mind set coming from Conscious Controlling Mind, which must be right at all costs.

Even if people have recovered their lost self and come to the point of Reparenting themselves, they can still be self righteous with subjects which they want to protect. It is all about protection, control, authority, safety and security. To feel safe, we have to be in control of our life. Unfortunately the opposite is true. When we feel all right about ourselves and self-validate, it does not make any difference if we are accepted or recognized because we know we are accepted since we recognize our own value. We do not need to be in control of the *situation* because we know we are in control of our *life*.

The key word is "need." If we *need* to have other people recognize us, the opposite will be true. People do not respond to need. In fact, people who are in control of their life will avoid people who are in need. (I am not talking about needy *hungry* people, but *emotionally* needy people.)

A good example of this was a person who staged a lecture for me. It went very well and more people showed up than she expected. But that is where it ended. I did not meet her expectations as to how I should perform. She had placed all her credibility on me performing as she thought I should. Within a short time, I could see that she was beginning to pick at me for items that were not relevant but she was setting up to blame me because she was getting some feedback which did not please her. This was her need to be in control and she was feeling uncomfortable because I did not perform as she expected me to.

When you are clear with yourself, you accept everything as it is and do not blame or complain. What other people do does not reflect on who you are. There are always going to be complainers. We cannot please some people no matter what we do. They see negative in everything because this is the way their life operates.

One of the major problems we have in communication is incongruent messages. If we are working from a place of not feeling good about ourselves, we will project this message out in what I call "meta-communication." It is a nonverbal, thought-based communication our mind sends out. Most people don't realize they are picking up the message, yet they will act on it without knowing why they are doing what they do. So it behooves us to clear the incongruent messages our mind is sending out ... and deleting all the files may take some work.

In *ReParenting* ourselves, we discover all the imprinted programs we received from our parents or other imprinters that set up the roles we play today. We have to get to the point of asking ourselves: "Whose life am I living? Am I living a replay of my parents or the life I choose to live?" Usually we find it is *not* the life we thought we were living. So where do we go from here?

How does it begin once we recognize we are in the wrong track and we are willing to switch back to the main-line? Since most of us (99%) experienced a traumatic incident in our childhood, we are not operating from true self since true self escaped into Magical Child to get away from the trauma. It makes no difference if it was real or just a perceived event. If the child created the experience, it was real to it.

When we escape and give up control, our mind's back-up system kicks in and sets up Conscious Controlling Mind and activates it. At the same time, it also activates autopilot to take control. At this point, you have lost control of your actions in your life. You did not know this so Conscious Controlling Mind begins controlling your life.

One or more split personalities took over your life using Conscious Controlling mind as the operating system. It is interested only in control, protection, security and safety. It will do whatever it must do to accomplish these end results. In small children, the main intent is to get attention, recognition and love. They will do whatever they need to do to get their needs met. This is the reason children act out. Parents do not understand the child's method of communication so they use their own interpretation, which tells them the child is acting out so they need to discipline it. This is based on the old dysfunctional control, authority and forced compliance parenting model.

When we remove the split personalities, we can begin to take control of our mind. This is the first step.

To begin with we must take control over our mind. To do this, we have a protocol with affirmations, or dialogues with our mind to get it working *with* us rather than against us. Going through these dialogues with your mind takes about an hour. We have discovered that some people have conflicts within their minds from trauma as a child, which will try to stop us from reclaiming control. If you have been operating on Autopilot for most of your life, Conscious Controlling Mind, or the autopilot operating system, will resist letting go of control. We can take control back by using the affirmations and once we do, we can reclaim control and begin to clear the cellular Memory.

To get to these programs, we must go through our mind's files like peeling an onion. Each layer will reveal another layer below it. When we peel most of them off, we begin to take control of our lives. As we move into more control, we can empower ourselves to work from a point of power rather than fear.

Once we have understood and can apply the concepts of the qualities of love to ourselves, we can apply them in our relationships with other people. It is almost amazing how people will respond to us when we have a congruent message coming from our own mind.

As we remove all the behavior patterns causing us to act out in the need for control, we find we do not need control any longer, since nobody is threatening us any longer. It was all a *perceived* threat, and not a *real* threat. We find we can cooperate with others, with no need to be in control. As we move into this new space of comfort, we find we begin to release stress. There really is no such thing as stress, but only stressed-out people. When you no longer react to the stress, it does not affect you.

As you move from a place of neediness, you begin to demand that people treat you differently. It is not that you become pushy or outwardly demanding of respect, but you just begin to avoid people who are not operating in your reality. It is almost as if you view the situation and, if it does not meet your needs, you drop it and move on with, "Next!" There is no need to make an issue out of it. If the shoe does not fit, discard it. You are now becoming more comfortable in your life, and it fits better, with no awkwardness. You have a lot more energy because you are not fighting with yourself to play a role.

At this point, you begin to recognize that most people play roles in their lives to meet their needs. Some of the major role pairs people play are: "Father/Daughter" and "Mother/Son." As you recover your lost self and grow up again, you can see how you fell into that role. Partnerships in these roles fall apart as soon as one partner begins to see they no longer want to play that role. If both partners can grow up, that's great, but it usually does not happen. In most cases, partners break up without ever finding out why the partnership did not work. They go out looking for a new partner, yet they find the same person in a different body and a different name, but with the same behavior patterns. Since they did not explore why the first relationship did not work, they end up in another ill-fated partnership again, which will fall apart due to not evaluating the situation that caused the breakup in the beginning. You must know the cause of the failure of the prior relationship before you embark on a new journey. You cannot play the blame game, as this does not reveal the cause of the breakdown. (We will discuss this topic in another book in this series.)

The main concepts we operate from that have been compromised and suppressed are self-esteem, self-worth and self-confidence. They are cluster qualities that cannot operate individually. We have them all or none. When I begin working with clients, I find their self qualities are operating at about zero to 20%, which means they do not see themselves as having much value. If we have never been given or shown what the seven qualities of love are, we will be trying to get them from outside ourselves. To get love, babies will push their parents to the limit but the parents do not know what it is so they get irritated and angry. In later years, the child gets sick to get attention. They assume any concentrated form of attention is love.

In the ReParenting process, we are releasing all the feelings of anger, fear, resentment and rejection locked into the body in the cellular memory. This is why talk therapy does not work; you cannot talk it out of the body. It must be removed from the Cellular Memory, which takes a special method. That's why Acupuncture is only marginally successful in dealing with emotional conflicts; the feelings are locked into the meridians and the muscle fiber. This creates pain as the muscles tighten up from the trauma locked into them from emotional experiences. There are a considerable number of points where this is locked in, which are diagrammed in Appendix A and B.

As we begin to remove locked-in emotional trauma, pain begins to lessen and we begin to feel better, as we recover the qualities which were denied to us in childhood.

Since most of us were never parented with a functional love program, we were not able to provide this program for our children so they need to be reparented, too.

Children need to respect and trust their parents, but they cannot do this until their parents Reparent themselves. I have been amazed by the changes in children when they catch on to the ReParenting process. It even works better if the children are given the opportunity to have a session where they can release all the negative feelings and emotions they are carrying.

The major stopping point in this Reparenting process is removing the cellular memory, which most therapists do not understand. Our body is our mind. All emotional trauma is deposited in the cellular facia tissue in the acupuncture points. The programs in our mind are located in our body not our brain. The brain is a control center switching network for the mind. This all explained in my books *Your Body Is Talking Are You Listening?* and *Energy Medicine – Energy Psychology.*

You can say all the affirmations and statements forgiving your parents and other people, but they very seldom will work unless you remove the anger and resentment from Cellular memory. It is the key to the ReParenting process.

With the help of a coach or a therapist, you *can* make major strides if the person you are working with has his or her own life together. It is unfortunate for the client that most practitioners went into the counseling field to find themselves, yet they did not know their own motivation. It is a sad statistic when we find that less than ten percent of the people in the counseling field are qualified to work in the field.

An excellent example of this came from a workshop I attended entitled Recovery for Therapists. Before I attended the workshop,

I thought I was on track as a good therapist. This workshop showed me why my issues kept coming up in sessions with clients.

At the beginning of the workshop, Wayne Gurtzberg handed out a questionnaire similar to what I had seen before. It was one in which you have to answer which alternative you would most likely or least likely do in the case of the question. For many of the questions, I would not do any, but you had to answer which one you do if you had to make a choice. Wayne said that he finds most people will not pass the grade as a effective therapist. He also said that he would probably throw out 35 percent of them because they were not being honest with themselves.

The questions had an interlock. If you answered a question a certain way, you had to answer the other questions in the same manner to line up properly. Out of the 101 people attending, he threw out 35 of the questionnaires that did not follow the profile and stated that only nine people were qualified to be effective therapists. He said, "You know who you are. If you are not in recovery work, you had better find yourself an objective therapist and start work on recovery."

I felt I had answered the questions accurately, and I was one of the nine. He then explained why we misdirect our clients. We do not want to bring up our own issues so we redirect them to something else which is non-threatening to us. This is the main failure point with most therapists. It explained why so many of my issues were coming up in sessions. Over the years it has helped me remove most of my issues. Needless to say I went home and contacted one of my friends so I could get to work recovering my lost self. It took many years to get clear. Now that I have done my work, I have cut recovering a client's lost self back to hours instead of years.

Very few people can make it over the grade without a mentor to help them, preferably one who has the experience of having gone through some of the same experiences you have had. There is a Native-American saying: "You cannot understand my life unless you have walked for a month in my moccasins."

Everybody has different experiences, yet they are all similar. Our mind is a very complex computer, and will make decisions for us until we take control back. Most of the time, the decisions are not what we would do if we had control, which is why I say most people have similar repeat experiences because everyone has the same mindset that makes the same decisions until we get control of it. There are only a limited number of experiences a person has. Everybody goes through the same basic experiences. Once we were able to get them cataloged, all we have to do is go to cause of that experience and we can clear it.

We require help in navigating through this process. As I stated, the 80-20 rule applies here too. Only 20% of the people recognize they are on a detour in their life. It takes courage to accept your life is not working and you have to take action now if you want to recover. Even with the 20% who recognize it, only 20% of them will take action and follow through. So where are we? If you take 100 people in our sample, only four will seek help, so we are not going get very far in this challenge. We have to stop this dysfunctional parenting model and change it to an effective functional family model.

Some people can do it alone, but it is very difficult and takes a lot of time ... and is not always successful. It is very hard to read your own book of life objectively. In fact much of it is blocked in denial so we do not have to go back through the pain and suffering. I use an affirmation I developed three years ago to allow the client's mind to release the files and bring them up. This is in a case history in the next chapter.

This whole process is detailed in the manual we use in sessions, *Energy Medicine/Energy Psychology: The Body/Mind Connection*, which has all the dialogues with our body/mind affirmations in it.

Now we have grown up, we can take our power back and start on the path to a new life. The choice is yours! Are you ready for peace, happiness, harmony, joy, unconditional love and abundance in your life? There are a lot of bridges to cross and many boulders to push out of the path, yet I know you can do if you apply yourself to the task.

8

Case Histories

I find that almost everybody needs to be ReParented. We are all looking for recognition and attention. "Any form of attention will do as long as I am noticed and you know I exist." This comes from children who are lost and feel they have no value. It does not come out of their mouth because many are afraid to say anything for fear they will be mistreated.

Deep down inside, we all want to be validated for who we are, which is why children act out. They now describe it as Radical Attachment Disorder (RAD). These children feel there is nobody they can trust so they act out to get attention. They do not know what any form of love is so they will take anything if you will respond to them. The problem is, we are again using the dysfunctional parenting model. Control, authority, discipline and compliance do not work. They never have.

Case history #1

Ten years ago, a fourteen-year-old boy was adopted from eastern Europe. He was diagnosed with a personality disorder coupled with RAD behavior which was in control as long as there were no confrontations that appear to cause rejection and loss of control. The confrontations were about anything he wanted but could not have. Other children teasing him would set him off too. He would go into a rage, with uncontrollable behavior. Obviously he was feeling rejected and never accepted. The adoptive parents divorced four years ago. The father really does not want to take care of the boy, which is obvious by his behavior and distant attitude toward the boy.

The boy had problems at school after his mother moved to an area she could afford. The father was a doctor so he had attended a school in a wealthy area. The children teased him and picked on him because he was not from their crowd. The mother was using forms of homeopathic remedies to control his behavior, which worked most of the time.

When the parents called me I was unaware they were divorced. The father was willing to go along with the psychiatrist who was recommending they send him into a controlled environment in a boys' boarding school because he had been arrested for going after the children who had been picking on him with a bull whip. However, this would have caused more rejection which would have aggravated the situation even more. The mother objected to this, but the school would not readmit the boy unless he kept taking the drugs.

The parents found my web site and emailed me to see if I was willing to work with their son. They were unsure of my claims, but after consulting with a few people I recommended, they call to validate my credentials. I then flew to their city to work with their son.

In four two hour sessions we had the child stabilized so he could understand his situation and function as a normal teenager. He took no more drugs, plus he was able to stop other children from picking on him.

The process proved itself out the following day. A month prior, the father had promised he would take his son to Yosemite Park for a week's vacation. He was looking forward to this adventure. The day after I finished working with him, his father called to say he was leaving the following day but he was not going take his son because he did not know what would happen with his son's behavior and he did not want to run into trouble. We explained to him what we had accomplished, yet I feel the father wanted treatment to fail so he could be proven right as he had in the past.

In the past, the child would have gone into uncontrollable rage, yet this did not happen. What was different? We had removed all the catalysts, triggers and activators that would have caused this reaction. We had released all the anger and fear programs which were attached to rejection and abandonment both by his birth parents and his adopted father.

I talked to his mother the following Monday. She was ecstatic with what we had accomplished. I also talked with the boy, who said he was very happy he was able to work with me. He did not react or act out in any way. It was as if he understood that his father was not there for him and he could not trust him. He said he did not want to live with his father anymore. I also did a session with his mother so she could function with congruent behavior so her son would know he could trust her. She was from a dysfunctional family, too, but was able to make full use of the functional parenting pattern. In the last nine months, he has not had problems or fallen back into his old behavior patterns. The mother says they get along great now since she is able to provide the seven qualities of love for him.

Case History # 2

A 31-year-old man from a dysfunctional family is currently living with both birth parents. He is in recovery from alcohol and drug addiction. He was born 10 years after his sister, an unexpected child. This caused the same result as the case history #1, due to his feeling rejected and abandoned. The parents weren't aware they were causing these interpretations for their child, as they had done the best they could. The interpretations were created before he was born due to the shock of being an unexpected child. The parents will not acknowledge this feeling of not being ready for a new child, so it has complicated the situation. All they would have to do is accept the situation and the mistake they made ... and ask for his forgiveness.

Very few parents will be honest about how they treated their children, because they cannot be honest with themselves. They really believe they overcame the reaction. The attitude is locked into their mind even though they block it out, but they resisted taking the opportunity to work out their issues. He grew up feeling on the outside, not accepted by the other children, and had a hard time adjusting in school. In college, he could not handle the stress of competition and ended up using alcohol to avoid the feelings and flunked out. He went from bad to worse with street drugs and found himself broke and living on street.

This is the result of RAD children who are not able to cope. Emotionally, he was stuck at 14 years old. If and when RAD children grow up, they can function in society again. Intervention and behavior modification did not work. He finally realized he had to get off drugs and alcohol yet was not stable enough to enter into society. His mother said she did not know what they were going to do with him until they met me. They had tried everything. If their life is not clear, they cannot help him, yet when he suggested they needed to work with me to help him, they decided not to do so.

He was hearing voices in his head and seeing illusionary visions. The doctor's diagnosis was bi-polar and possibly manic-depressive syndrome. His brain/mind was malfunctioning from the escape into magical child. The neuro-transmitters in his brain were not functioning properly.

In sessions, we cleared up much of it to this point, and he is functioning fairly well now. This is an ongoing case with a lot more to work out. I have my doubts that he will continue with this process so we can clear him up. He has not made any further appointments with me and continues in his inability to cope with life very well. Generally I have discovered we must get the situation cleared before a teenager is 16. After age 16, the programs are locked in, which makes it very hard and complex to clear.

Case history #3

The family appears to be a loving supportive family who cares for their children very well. It would seem as if it they are a functional family. In the long run, however, it did not play out in a positive manner. The children are now in their late 30s and 40s, and are having behavioral problems with their own children.

In this case, a 45-year-old man came to my lecture. He was a good looking guy yet he had the voice of a ten-year-old. When we evaluated this, he did not know or understand why this had happened. I used Kinesiology (muscle testing) to talk with his Subconscious Mind, and we discovered a traumatic experience at 10 years old which blocked his emotional development.

I have never worked with an adult or child who was this adept to figure out what his parents were doing. It appeared he had received total acceptance, approval and unconditional love from his parents. They always supported him and gave him acceptance for every paper or artwork he brought home from school. He received excellent grades on everything.

He decided to test his parents so he drew a piece of artwork that was poorly done. He asked his teacher if he had handed it in at school would he have received a failing grade on it. She said, "I hope you are not going to turn it in." He gave it to his mother and she responded in the same enthusiastic manner she did with everything he had brought home. That crashed his life. He then knew what they were doing was what they thought was the proper behavior, but it was hollow and had no meaning. His feeling was, 'They really don't care. They're living in an illusion and doing what is right but it doesn't mean anything." His trust of them was broken, and he grew up with his interpretation about love which was "Indifference. My parents do not really care for me." This was proven out over the next ten years.

His grades dropped and he did not have much motivation to succeed. He tried college and dropped out. He finally found a small business at age 24 which really interested him so he asked the owner if he could trade time for some of the company's products. He then became a parachute designer and now owns most of a multi-million dollar company which he runs. The problem was that when people called him on the phone, they would ask to speak to his father because his voice sounded like a child.

We cleared this all up by forgiving, accepting and loving his parents, knowing they had one the best they could under the circumstances. He released all the anger and resentment from his body. We reprogrammed his view and interpretation about love and his voice dropped three octaves from a high alto to a baritone. We had cleared all the programs which locked him in at age 10, so he could grow up emotionally. This changed his whole life. His family now related with him in a positive manner, because they knew he could give them love. His wife was so impressed with his recovery she made an appointment and now they have a functional family.

We will always attract into our life people who demonstrate the substitute form of love we have accepted. As result, the lesson goes on and on until we recognize it.

Both he and his wife had accepted indifference as love, so they treated each other with indifference, which was devastating to their children. With a functional form of unconditional love, they now communicate in a totally functional manner which is supportive for their children. It has also put their marriage back on the right track so they can stay together

Case history #4

Children are very easy to work with, as they do not have a lot of locked-in behavior patterns. They are very open and quite resilient. They bounce back quickly when they catch on to what I am doing. When they can feel the anger and resentment leaving their body, they will begin to trust and accept that what we are working with is practical.

I saw a 12-year-old boy who had been adopted at age 5 from Russia. He is a very intelligent boy, but had reactionary problems. The school stated that if the parents refused to give him Ritalin, the child would be suspended because he was too disruptive in the classroom.

We released all the rejection and abandonment from his birth parents and the situation at the orphanage in Russia where he did not receive much attention. When we were able to build trust in him by releasing all the resentment and anger from his experiences, he came around very well.

He was very resistant with his adoptive parents because he did not know if he would be rejected again, as this had been the pattern from his early childhood experiences in Russia. He had a fear of intimacy and commitment, so he held his adoptive parents at arm's length and would not let them get close to him because he did not trust them do to the prior programming (a common behavior with adopted children). It was very frustrating for them because they wanted a child they could be loving and affectionate with, but he would not let them in, so they felt they had made a mistake in adopting him.

After the session with me, he warmed up to his adoptive parents and would allow them to hug him, He became very close to them, his grades at school improved and his behavior was no longer a problem, as he fitted in very well at school.

He asked his asked his mother when I was coming to Orlando again because he wanted to see me again. This vindicated the parents, knowing they had made the proper decision to bring him to a session with me, as his behavior was now normal and he could get along with his classmates very well. The RAD behavior was gone permanently.

I use my definition of RAD behavior, which is based on my experience working with this dysfunction. When you change their attitude about who they are and release the fear, anger and resentment about rejection and abandonment, the RAD behavior is eliminated and disappears forever.

RAD behavior is caused by inability to trust and feeling you can't get close to anybody for fear of rejection. The more intense the feeling of rejection and mistrust, the more children act out in survival. They act out because this is the only way they know how to get attention. It would seem totally opposite to an effective way to get attention but when you have been rejected all your life, negative attention is a form of love substitute. They feel people are indifferent to them and do not care even if they *do* care. When you are in the illusion of fear of intimacy and commitment, you push everyone away out of fear. When we release all the rejection and abandonment issues, plus all the resentment with love and forgiveness, and untangle their childhood and letting go of the activators, triggers and catalysts for the RAD behavior, the problem disappears forever. This ReParenting session worked very well.

Case history #5

The type of clients I really like to work with are totally open and ready to go with no considerations of my credentials. A person called me, telling me she'd read my book in two days, and she knew I was her ticket out of pain.

When she arrived, she said, "I don't care how long it takes or how much it costs; let's get started." We were dealing with major back and neck pain problems caused by the dysfunctional parenting program. Asking questions with kinesiology was not new to her, but the way I asked questions was. We were able to get to an understanding of why all the programs and patterns of the past had become active in the last five years. As we worked on releasing the pain, she was amazed that you could talk it out by holding acupuncture points. In the two days we worked together, we changed her life so significantly her friends and colleagues wanted to know if she could get me to come to their town. I did and the rest is history. I have been there many times. We have a great ongoing relationship now. She has done many sessions with me, which have taken her from almost total disability to massive success in her business. This has been one of the most successful ReParenting processes I have ever accomplished. It shows us that you can come from almost total failure to great success in less than two years.

Case history #6

This client works for a Fortune 500 company, but she knew her company was going through rough times during the Dot Com crash in 2001. She said, "I do not have any pain or disability in my body. I feel I have programs and beliefs that are sabotaging me, which may cost me my job because they are cutting back and laying people off like crazy. I do not want to lose my job so getting me geared up to succeed is very important. I can only see you once a month unless I cut back on my expenses."

When she saw the chips were down as her department was going from 54 people down to 14, she decided to see me more often. To do this moved out of her house into a house with another person in her office near work so she did not have to spend money on gas. She stopped smoking and limited her evenings out. She came to see me every time I was in my office in Silicon Valley. Her office staff then went down to seven. At this point we had released all the childhood programming and had recovered the seven qualities of love. All her childhood anger and resentment was cleared, so we worked on empowering her to stand up and say what she needed to say and stand up for herself.

This was a major step in the ReParenting process since she had always been negated and invalidated by her parents. Her relationships never really bloomed because she had fear of intimacy and fear of commitment. She always seemed to choose the little boys who were safe because she was a controller, but these were not satisfying or successful relationships. We put that on the side until she felt comfortable in being in conversation with the management of her company. She did not want to feel fear of them or not be able to communicate in a meeting. She was climbing up the management ladder since her department had closed and she'd been promoted. When her supervisor was laid off, I told her, "Make herself indispensable so they need your services. You do not need to 'brown nose' to get noticed; just be effective in your work." She did and when they decided they had the core group to move forward, she was included.

We cleared up all the relationship conflicts and she was ready to fly. She did just that as she became an administrative assistant to one of the sales directors. She asked if she could move to Phoenix and then asked if she could work out of her home and move near Sedona. They wired her house up so she could work at home. She is now in middle management. She moved from an assistant to a local sales group to a nationwide administrative assistant for two upper management company sales directors. In ten years, she went from an income of $18,000 a year to $60,000 a year. She never thought she would ever have a new car or be able to buy a home and do some traveling. Now she has all three. Last time I saw her, she was sailing free with no conflicts.

Case history #6

"I was a prisoner in my body. I contracted polio when I was fourteen. I was in an iron lung for a year and was unable to walk. I spent five years in a wheelchair until I was able to learn how to walk. For the last 25 years, I have dragged my feet, unable to lift my legs. I had considered suicide because I don't really have a life. Dr. Art challenged me with an offer I could not resist. He said, 'If I can't clear the Polio symptoms that cause your disabilities there will be no cost to you. If I do release them so you can walk normally then the fee is double.' I could not resist the double or nothing because I did not think he could do it. In less than two hours, he found the causes and I walked out his office normally. After spending $30,000 for nothing $500 was a real steal. I got my life back."

– Janet S., Elk Grove, CA

This was a very interesting session because she did not think I could clear her disability of thirty years. We discovered she was an only child from a relatively functional family until she was age six.

Then problems began with the birth of her brother, who received all the recognition and acceptance, with her left on the side line. Her parents paid no attention to her; it was as if she was not there. Her brother became the super student, star little league player and the super soccer player. She tried getting sick to get attention from 12 to 14, which did get her some attention. At fourteen, she contracted Polio, which put her in an iron lung for almost a year. She had to learn how to walk again and was in a wheelchair for five years. Her attempt to get love, attention and recognition worked but what a price to pay for the next 30 years. In this case, it was easy to ReParent her because she had the foundation. We only had to forgive her parents and brother, and release all the anger and resentment she had locked up in her body. Bingo! She could walk again, and it only took one session!

Case history # 7

"I had diabetes, which was causing my eyesight to deteriorate. Even though I knew what caused it, I could not stop it. It becomes even more of a conflict since I work at a medical college and the doctors could not do anything for me. When Dr. Art began to check it out, we found the diabetes, but diabetes was not the root cause. We went back further and discovered that it was my need for love, attention, recognition and approval when I was a child that caused the diabetes. Since I did not want to address the issue of anger with my parents, it was telling me I had look at the issue. Not only that, I had married a man who was a duplicate of my father. When we cleared the issues with my family and my husband by forgiving them, releasing my anger and resentment with love and forgiveness, my eyesight was restored and my diabetes was gone."

–Myra Recovachecyk, Toronto, Canada

This was a very interesting series of sessions. In the second session, we had the diabetes cleared but we could not get the eyesight to clear up. I called one of my practitioners to ask her if she would call Myra and question her to find out what was blocking our ability to clear her eyesight. We found out her mind had totally locked down in denial all the information that was causing her eyesight problems. She asked me to develop an affirmation that would allow her mind to release the information locked in her body.

I told her, "If we can't release the programs causing your eyes to continue to deteriorate, you will not have to pay me for the session. If I do succeed, then you will have to pay the normal session fee." She agreed and we accomplished getting her eyesight back for her. It was all about anger and resentment at her parents and her husband, who was a replacement for her parents.

So ReParenting involves going back and reclaiming the personal power you lost as a child, and loving and forgiving your parents for not providing the seven qualities of love. Then you must reclaim unconditional love for yourself.

Case history #8

Children are our major challenge in life as they are so adept between ages two and seven. We have to be very careful what we say in their presence, as they just absorb everything we say. They learn by example, too. Most of the people I work with have had conflicts between the ages of two and eight.

This story begins at a very young age and continues up until I saw him when he was age 35. He was very adept and received good grades in school. School was very easy for him, so he began bringing home papers and report cards which threatened his parents. He was too smart for them to handle so they did not pay any attention to things he brought home. Most of their responses were, "You did alright," or, "You could have done better," without even noticing what he brought home.

He was the valedictorian of his senior class and graduated with a 4.0 average. He went to college on a scholarship and graduated magna cum laud with an MBA. With all this, you would assume he would really succeed. He took a job with a local bank. After two years, he was offered a position as a loan officer. Two weeks after he took the job, he had a grand mal seizure. What led up to this and why would he have this happen to him when everything up until now had worked well?

The answer goes back to how his parents treated him and the opinion he had of himself. Even though he had all the mechanics to succeed, his belief in himself was lacking. The seeds were set in place during his childhood. When he took a position with responsibility, his mind freaked out. It went back to his files and reviewed them. His cybernetic system activated the Amygdala and it set up a seizure to stop him from working in this position. His mind did not feel he could handle the job.

When you do not have control of your mind, it will control you, so we went through the standard procedures of release – parents and all the childhood programs – so we could empower him to recognize his abilities ... and he hit the wall again. His wife was a controller; they had a Mother/Son relationship. When he was able to claim his power, his wife invented a flimsy excuse and divorced him. He was growing up after I worked with him on ReParenting him. He had another seizure while being rejected by his wife. I saw him a few more times and put him back on his feet again. I am not sure what happened from there on. The main conflict he had was rejection.

Case history #9

A woman came to my lecture, pleading, "Can you help me pass the California teacher credential test? I've given up on taking the credential test, having failed it six times, with no idea why."

We discovered why she was failing the tests, although it did not make sense to her. Her father and husband had programmed her to fail! That was a revelation for her. First, we released being rejected by her mother before she was born. Then we went through the same Reparenting process and released all the anger and resentment at her father and her husband. I told her not to study at all, and that she knew all she need to know since she had been working as a teacher for 15 years. She came in the day before the exam, and I showed her how to take a multiple choice test and helped pump her self-esteem and confidence. She passed in the 94th percentile. Before, she had never finished the test. She finished with 45 minutes to spare.

Our interpretation of our value is so important, we have to make sure nobody has attacked it . If they have, we must empower ourselves to reclaim our personal power.

Case history # 10

He had been diagnosed as a classic case of learning-disabled, coupled with ADD. His family had sent him to many therapists but to no avail. At their suggestion, he enrolled in a college that helped learning-disabled people, but after five years, he was still in his junior year. He was listless, and had difficulty getting out of bed each morning and just making it through the day.

As usual, his problems all stemmed from childhood during which he collected the usual rejection programs in addition to his father continually putting him down. He did poorly in school, and was unable to fit into the social scene. When his school labeled him learning-disabled, he bought it hook, line and sinker.

In the first session, we cleared the ADD label and learning-disabled belief, along with all the traditional programs. Immediately, he began to find school easier. He was amazed that we could release pain in his body and change his programming and belief by just holding acupuncture points on the body and saying an affirmation. Over two more sessions, he reclaimed his personal power and took responsibility back, and perked up in every area of his life. He is now eager to tackle each day, and wants to be up and around. He tells me, "I've never felt like this before. Now I have this drive to succeed and get going in my life." A classic example of a young man who was raised not to believe in himself. He accepted everything that was said about him. He grew up feeling he was a failure and would never amount to anything. When he went through the ReParenting process, he realized he has control of his life. He was not the dumbbell everybody was telling him he was.

Case history #11

A client lived only a few blocks from my office, and was a virtual prisoner in his house. He was afraid to go out due to what he described as "environmental illness"; he felt he was allergic to everything.

We began with his pre-birth rejection by his mother – she didn't want any children. She verbally and physically abused him, and wore strong perfume all the time, so he connected rejection and abuse with strong perfume. With a shy victim-type personality, it was no surprise when he married a strong, controlling woman who verbally abused him and controlled his life. He was seeking a mother-son relationship so that he could continue to work out relationship lessons with his mother. His wife also wears strong perfume, which is the core issue. He finally built up the courage to break up with his wife, which left him alone, a prisoner in his own mind.

He had worked at a scientific laboratory that used strong-smelling chemicals – the catalyst. He developed reactions to the chemicals, and finally retired on disability. His allergy syndrome built on itself until he was afraid to go anywhere.

First, we cleared all the childhood programming with his mother. Then we cleared all the programs about abuse by his ex-wife. After that we tackled the beliefs and programs driving the concepts about environmental illness. It took three sessions to finally clear everything. Once clear, he offered to pay me to go to a lecture with a person he had wanted to go for years but was afraid to leave his home. We took a field trip to a lecture to try out his newfound freedom.

As fate would have it, a woman with strong perfume sat down right behind us, and he bolted for the door to get some fresh air. Outside, I managed to convince him that his environmental sensitivity is a self-created illusion, and we went back in to enjoy the rest of the lecture. Over the next few sessions, we cleared his remaining problems, finally releasing him to find happiness and joy for the first time in his life.

Quite often there is a catalyst that activates a condition. We think the condition is real because of the way we feel and suffer from it. The fear causes us to shut down. As you can see in this case it was his mother's abuse of him that placed the seeds in his mind which caused the problem. Yet they did not sprout until he had been married for many years. Finally the bombs went off and his mind attached it to strong odors and fragrances. When we were able to regain control of his mind so it was not controlling him, forgive his mother and his ex-wife for their abusive behavior, he was able to recover his self-esteem, self-worth and self-confidence. It is so critical to recover the seven qualities of love that he lost during childhood so he could recover his lost self and get back on his feet and live a normal life. The ReParenting process works on any malfunction that is keeping us from living a normal life.

When we revert to our childhood programming, it takes over (as his did) and makes us a prisoner in our own mind. We do not know this is happening because we do not have control over our mind's functions. Our mind thinks it is protecting us and making us safe, yet we can see this man was suffering and struggling with a belief that was not real.

Case history #12

When we are dealing with out-of-control children, the books on dealing with the reactive child are not approaching discipline in the proper manner. It is not about authority, control, manipulation and demanding compliance to our rules. Here is a good example.

I saw a 19-year-old man who had been arrested for running drugs. He'd been at the wrong place at the wrong time. His friend was the drug runner he had been getting his drugs from. When he went to court they decided to put him on probation if he would spend 30 days in a drug rehab center. His father found one that was more spiritually oriented so he made the reservation. I was in the area where the center was, so his father made an appointment with me to work with him before he dropped him off. He had been diagnosed with bi-polar mental disability, anxiety, severe anger syndrome and a few others.

In the first session, we went through the basic Reparenting processes to get his mind in control and release some of the anger. Bi-polar is the mind being out of control and not being able to make accurate viable decisions. When we gained control over his mind, the bi-polar disappeared. We did not get all the anger at his mother cleared in the first session.

When he entered the rehab center, the staff were surprised that all the conditions listed on the psychiatrist's report did not seem to be present now. After two weeks, his father received permission to take him out for three hours for another session with me. We finished clearing all the anger at his mother and worked with all the causes for anxiety and all the childhood conflicts that had resulted in his using drugs to run away from himself.

All the children I have worked with who get on drugs are brilliant children who feel lost and have no value. Self-rejection is one of the basic causes in this and in most cases where the child feels mother does not care for them. Love becomes (in their mind) indifference; nobody really cares. In this young man's case, his parents were divorced and mother had custody. It would have been much better if he had lived with his father who understood his situation.

On his return to the rehab center, he was asked to do another evaluation of his progress. The results of the conference were very interesting. He was asked a few questions, but he really surprised them with this response. "My progress is not at all about what you are doing here. You are using the wrong approach. It is not about authority and control, complying with your discipline at all. It is about respect, trust, approval, validation and recognition coupled with unconditional love, acceptance and forgiveness. I know that is your intention but you are not using practicing properly."

The psychiatrist, director and the others on the panel were stunned by his response. They decided to put him in as a group leader because they could see he was quite clear. It only took two sessions to ReParent him and clear years of mistreatment and set a new goal in his life.

The methods we use to deal with reactive children do not work. This young man's problems were the result of the basic dysfunctional parenting model of control, authority and compliance. He is now doing well and is balanced in his life, according to his father who he is living with now. He called his mother and let her know how he felt about her and what had happened to him. He said, "Do not call me. If I need something from you, I will call you."

Case history # 13

Earlier I said we draw to us the perfect partner to learn the lesson we need to accomplish. This is why it is so critical to ReParent ourselves so we can be clear of all the skeletons in our closet. If we don't, they will start rattling at some time in our relationship.

Here is a good example of not being able to see what you are attracting. A women came to see me with the complaint: "I finally am seeing I attracted an adult child as my husband. Where were you twenty years ago when I was out prospecting for a husband?"

Unfortunately I was not in her town. She is finally recognizing this relationship has not worked for over ten years in retrospect. She tells her husband she is *not* his mother which he does not even understand.

It took many sessions to unwind this relationship. What we discovered was that her religious training was conflicting with her desire to have a functional relationship. We had to deal with it first so she could lay it on the line to her husband that he had six months to wake up and make the relationship work. Needless to say, he did not know how to do it even after he done two sessions with me. As a result she divorced him, which caused a lot of conflict for her, since she had two children she had to deal with. Once she was divorced, she began her search for another relationship. However, she kept drawing in adult children. She knew the reasons why she had done so in the past.

We had many sessions and worked on Reparenting many times. What was wrong? After much work on the belief and program, we found that her mother had imprinted her with many beliefs about how men were ruthless and took advantage of women. The independent types were zeroed in by her mother: "They will take advantage of you. What you need is a nice supportive man when you grow up."

All this was input when she was very young. Her mother was a controller and her father was very meek and would not stand up to her mother at all. The stage was set for the nice, safe, supportive man by her mother. She did not even remember her mother saying this. It was in the Subconscious mind's database and was controlling her decisions and choices of men in her life.

Our mind will actually make decisions for us and set up choices which are in line with its programs and beliefs ... and we do not even know this is happening. You can only make choices based on what is presented to you. Her mind was looking for a particular type of person. Even when she used Internet dating services, the same type of person would always show up. Needless to say, after four relationships, she was frustrated. We were able to find the above imprinting by her mother and remove it totally ... and the picture changed radically immediately. We had cleared the fear of intimacy and fear of commitment over a year earlier but this series of programs was haunting her and we could not find them until she brought up a situation she did not understand and it opened the door to clearing the challenge in relationships.

Case history #14

From the stories I hear, it seems that a good majority of parents are totally frustrated on how to handle the reactive child. It is very hard to deal with intervention when a child is acting out if you have not Reparented yourself. Children are in the need of unconditional love, trust and respect. They want to know they are safe and protected. How can they feel this if their parents cannot offer them unconditional love. Again, if you do not have it, how are you going to offer it?

My wife grabbed my granddaughter when she was acting out and would not let go. She held her for over fifteen minutes, telling her she was safe. "I am giving you love and accepting you as you are. You are alright. I want you to know I am here to protect you. You are safe. I am not going to discipline you. I want you to know I am here for you so you can calm down now."

After fifteen minutes, she finally came to her senses and calmed down. Her mother will not let me go through the Reparenting process with her, yet her daughter goes out of control when she feels she is not getting what she wants. My son can be the intermediary if he is there, but many times, he cannot step in if he is not there. Even if he is there, sometimes she goes out of control. Our other granddaughter is in control of herself and seems to handle herself very well in all situations without any help.

Case history #15

A mother who was a friend of my wife came to me with an interesting challenge. Her son was wetting his bed at seven years old. And the school wanted her to give him Ritalin or they were going to expel him for disrupting his class.

How do you work with a person who does not believe in my process and is skeptical I can accomplish anything? She has taken him to a child psychologist and a doctor, but they could offer nothing except drugs.

It is interesting how children will talk to me and tell me the truth of how they feel. The reason is they can trust me and they know I will be honest with them. How do they know that? They pick it up from me intuitively. Their mind will allow me to communicate with them with no conflicts because they trust me. This has proven out with every child I have worked with.

What he told me was that he felt rejected by his mother. I had to engage him in conversation to get him to begin talking with me. His father did not give him any time at all for he was caught up in his work and other activities.

This child was seven years old. Does this seem amazing that I could talk with him at this level? His parents were not able to talk with him. I usually tell parents I cannot do much with children over the long haul unless I do a session with the mother too. In this case, she was not willing to do a session with me. She felt I should be able to work with her son if my process works. It was a challenge to see if I could accomplish my goal. I made a deal with him: if his mother would provide love and recognition for him, he would stop wetting his bed.

When he felt she was not paying attention to him, he could ask her for love and support. She agreed to our deal and he stopped wetting his bed. The next step was the Reparenting so he could feel he was accepted and would stop rejecting himself. We removed all the fear that his mother was not there for him and reinstalled the love program.

We had to work on forgiving his sister for pushing him out so he was not in competition with her for mom's love any more. When we accomplished setting up a new reality for him so he was able to work in school without acting out any longer because he knew that all the rejection he felt was his own perception. (When children set up a perception they are being rejected, they apply it across the board, so they pull back assuming everybody is rejecting them.)

In a very short while, he became adjusted to this new reality with other children and everything worked for him. It is interesting that his mother did not give me any feedback. She was surprised it worked. Sometimes I feel that parents are secretly upset that I can change a child's behavior and make it work. In some case they are upset that I could make it work and they could not.

Case history #16

A mother brought her daughter to see me because she was failing in school. She thought moving her to a private school would help since she would get more individual attention, but this did not seem to help. She had been adopted, which was the main conflict. She had no self-esteem, self-worth or self-confidence. She saw herself as a failure in her life. It seemed like everything was against her. She had been in an orphanage for four years before she was adopted. Her mother was a streetwalker as they described her at the time of adoption. She had been taken away from her mother when she was less than six months old.

At the first session, I found she was trying to prove to her mother that she made a mistake in adopting her. This was at twelve years old. The conflicts had been going on for eight years. Her mother was at her wit's end. She was asking herself why she brought a child like this into her life. What was she trying to learn from this? Quite often I find people who are trying to be do-gooders and help out an orphan child have the situation blow up in their face because they did not know what they were getting into, since they really do not know the child's back ground. They get a sketchy description at the time of adoption. The adoption agencies in eastern Europe are appreciative to find a home for children they had in orphanages for extended lengths of time.

Mother is enthralled to find a child because she could not find one in the states. All adopted children, no matter where they are from, have fear of intimacy and fear of commitment. She found all the attention and support she gave her daughter did not work because adopted children will not let you get close to them for fear of repeated rejection. This is a safety protection system their mind has so they will not be disappointed again. It takes about ten to twelve years to get past this one under normal circumstance. In the ReParenting process, we can get through it one or two sessions.

We cleared out all the rejection from birth mother and feeling that 'nobody is there for me.' There was an intense amount of self-rejection, all locked into the cellular memory so there is no way any form of verbal counseling will remove it. The mother found this out in many attempts to work with a child psychologist. When we got to the core of the issues, we found that the child had such a low self-image of herself she could not see how anybody could help her. As always I find children will trust and accept me so we can make fast progress. As we were able to peel all the negative attitudes and beliefs off, she started coming around and feeling better. She was able to sleep better and the nightmares and scary dreams disappeared. We were making progress. She was succeeding at school now that she had a better self-image. Her mother could now begin to provide unconditional love and recognition for her. The key here was that her mother did the Reparenting process with me to remove all her dysfunctional childhood programs which were blocking the child's feeling about getting close to mother. "You can't provide what you do not have," I told her.

Once the mother was able to understand what love was, she was able to provide love and recognition, so the child began warming up to her. Now that we have worked both with mother and daughter, the child is now doing very well in school since she has recovered her self-worth, self-esteem, self-confidence and self-image. She now knows she has value as a person. You have to be able to validate yourself before anyone will see that in you. This is the ReParenting process shining in the best application.

Afterthoughts

What is ReParenting then?

My approach is recovering our lost self that we lost in child-hood due to traumatic experiences which caused us to run away from ourselves and hide. We really were not hidden; we just shielded ourselves from what we thought we were afraid of. We were still quite visible, yet we could not feel the perceived fear.

Unfortunately the chain reaction we created in our mind caused us to lose control of our life. The seeds that were set in place in our mind by the experiences with our parents did not sprout until we were adults. Many times they became time bombs that set off a whole series of reactions we had no control over since we did not know what the causes, catalysts, triggers and activators were.

Since mother did not know what love was, she could not pro-vide it for us. However, we reacted, assuming she knew what it was and *should* be providing it for us but was withholding. When we did not get it from her, we became angry and pushed her for love and recognition, which we did not get because she could not understand our language. We only had one method but it did not work because mother became irritated by our behavior. As a re-sult we decided we were not alright, not accepted, not recognized and began to self-reject because we were feeling the rejection from mother.

You must be authentic. You cannot give or provide what you do not have. In other words, you cannot provide unconditional love if you do not have it yourself. Until it is reinstalled in your mind through the ReParenting process, you do not have it. In my experience, less than two percent of the adults today have unconditional love installed in their mind which also means that less than two percent of the adults today came from functional families.

Unfortunately, we never grew up with a functional parenting program which provided the seven qualities of unconditional love. We were subjected to the dysfunctional control, authority and compliance model, which does not work.

The result is reactionary children, introverted children, and many other dysfunctional behavior patterns, all of whom have very little self-esteem, self-worth and self-confidence.

There are the exceptions who seem to be able to weather the storm of dysfunctional families, break away and succeed in their lives no matter what mistreatment they suffered as child. They are in the minority, though.

So how do we stop this dysfunctional parenting program which is being passed on and handed down from generation to generation? In my books, I have written how I did it by recognizing the challenge and meeting it head on. And also by not having children until we felt we had overcome our programs which were dysfunctional from our childhood. We stopped in our family. How about you?

Remember how earlier in the book, I said, "If you have resistance to any of the statements, examples, or case histories or what you may feel you have done in your family, read it again to see if you were able to understand my intent."

I would like to have your input as to what you feel is missing, a mistake or something not emphasized enough.

email me at: mailforart@gmail.com

With Love on your journey, Art Martin, April, 2009

Appendices

Appendix A: N/CR Questions and Answers

Q: What comprises an N/CR Session?

A: We will be working with Neuro/Cellular Reprogramming, Behavioral Kinesiology, and biofeedback, if necessary. We demonstrate methods to understand the dialogue, misperceptions, interpretations and programs that the Subconscious Mind has stored in cellular memory. We use Kinesiology (muscle testing) to access programs and sub personalities and get a general direction regarding what we have to clear. The acupuncture points on the body are switches or gates. Putting pressure on these entry points turns on the mind's "VCR" and opens the dialogue with the Subconscious Mind's files so that we can release the programs.

We must resolve certain basic issues before we can begin the process:

1. The client must be anchored in the body. Many people are out of their body and are unaware they are not functioning in their body, especially if they are confronting a traumatic issue. However, once they know how it feels, they can recognize when this has happened.

2. Electrical polarity must be correct in order for Kinesiology to work properly. If the polarity is reversed, "yes' will appear as "no" and "no" as "yes." We cannot

obtain an accurate answer until polarity is balanced properly.

3. Therapists must be in recovery to set up the Unconditional Love file in their mind so they can love themselves. If we do not have unconditional love installed in our mind, we cannot be an effective therapist. Separation from Source will cause a lack of love, along with self-rejection. We must accept our entitlement to love.

4. We must find out if the three lower minds are going to work with us. If not, then we must rewrite and reprogram the files and write new scripts. We must get Ego to recognize that we are not going to destroy it, and to convince it to be our friend.

At this point, we are now ready to ask questions with Kinesiology, or go directly into program releases. We can go directly to the root causes and the core issues stored in the Subconscious Mind's files. This will reveal the programs that have become habit patterns that are causing dysfunctional behavior, illness, diseases or pain in any form. We can quickly release and heal any dysfunctional program using N/CR. *(See steps in a session in chapter 15 for the protocol for the process described in "Your Body is Talking; Are You Listening?)*

I recommend recording all sessions for the protection of both therapist and client. Also, the session can be reviewed and transcribed. There will be many parts of the session the client will not be able to recall because the mind may block it out. Many people have found that repeating the affirmations will lock in the new programming.

Q. **Why is this particular process so effective?**

A. Unlike other therapy processes, the client is required to participate in the session. The client is not *worked on*. In most treatments, such as Rolfing, Trager, massage, acupuncture, and other body-related processes, you do not participate. In psychology, you will be asked what your problem is, but few clients know what the base and root cause is, so how can we work with a belief, concept, or a program when we are not sure of the cause? The body will always reveal the base causes and the core issues if we listen to it.

We must get Middle Self to cooperate with us, as it is one of the main players in the game. The Middle Self knows exactly what is happening in our life, so we need its support. All levels are brought in to play, physical, emotional, mental, spiritual and etheric, all at the same time. The body being a hologram, we access all levels of the mind and body with Kinesiology and with clairvoyance to access the records that we need in releasing the programs. We go one further by accessing the ability of the Higher Self to go to the akashic records for past life information. Any malfunction in a person life at any level can be cleared up. There are no limitations. We must release programs at the Subconscious level from the data base files, archive files and the denial files. We are not just releasing the charge which causes pain or dysfunction.

Q. **What should you expect during a treatment?**

A. To understand what a treatment is like, you must first understand what it is not like. No special preparations or clothing are required. You will not experience any deep tissue work that is painful, nor will you be required to accept altered states of consciousness. We do not use hypnosis or guided imagery. You will not be expected to dredge up painful, emotional experiences from the past or "lead the discussion" as in analytical psychology. In fact, you do not need to tell us anything. Your body will reveal all we need to know, although we may ask some questions to establish some basic criteria. It's easier to access programs if you make up a list of the basic issues you would like to cover. This way, we can focus on the issues you want work on.

Emotions may come up and you may experience flashbacks during the process but they are all momentary and release quickly.

We use affirmations as the means to reprogram and rewrite scripts in the mind. The therapist creates the affirmation, then the client repeats the affirmation. The affirmations are software for the mind. The only person that can reprogram your mind is you; there is no such person as a healer of others. You can only heal yourself. As such, we are only facilitators to direct the process.

Q. What goes on during a treatment?

A. When we began this work in the 1980s, we jumped in and started releasing programs from the body. As we progressed through the years, we found we had to take control of our mind so we developed affirmations we now describe as "dialogues with the mind." These can take up to an hour to take control of your mind.

When we locate the cause or core issue with Kinesiology,

we must determine if it is a belief or reality. If it's only a belief, it may be controlled by a sub-personality. In either case, we can release it with an affirmation that will reprogram the software. If it is body-based, then we have to locate the acupuncture point that holds the incident we are releasing; a momentary pain will occur at that point. As we bring up details of the incident and forgive the cause, it will disappear immediately.

We do not experience the mind's action during the process; it instantly communicates to the body through neurosynapses and signals the muscles to let go of the tension. At the same time, it is rewriting the programs in the computer. Through affirmations, we communicate what we want to happen. It is important to understand that you are giving permission and removing the programs yourself. As the therapist leads you through the affirmation, you are healing your own body. The therapist is actually just a facilitator who has agreed to let you release the negative energy through him/her, providing an opportunity to experience love and forgiveness to release the incident.

Q. How long does this take and how much does it cost?

A. The number of treatments depends on your willingness to let go. Taking responsibility to see life differently without judgment, justification, rejection or fear/anger helps. A typical average is three to ten sessions. Some clients have had over 100 sessions, while others have cleared most of their issues in four to ten. There have been miracles in one session, but they are rare.

The cost of a session is $125 per hour. Sessions are two

hours. Call (800) 655-3846 or call our office at (916) 663-9178. If you do not get a call back within 24 hours, then call our cell phone (916) 710-6413 for an appointment. Check our website at: www.transformyourmind.com for our schedule. If you are interested in spreading the word of this work please call us. We would be happy to work with you. We are setting up a network of practitioners that will be listed on our website.

Q. **How can I become a sponsor?**

A. If you would like to help us present lectures or introductory workshops, please call the number above. We provide a free session if you set up a lecture for us (a minimum of ten people). If you are interested in setting up appointments for me at a designated location I will provide you with a free session for each day I work at your location (there is a minimum numbe r of sessions each day to qualify). We teach the Energy Psychology Neuro/Cellular Repatterning process in a five workshop series. If you would like to sponsor a workshop we allow you to attend free.

Appendix B: How the Mind Functions

The human mind is a tool for transformation provided that we use it properly. Contrary to popular belief, there is more to our mind than brain researchers have found. Some psychologists divide mind into the Conscious and Unconscious minds. Others refer to the Subconscious Mind, which is the appropriate description because it is far from the dictionary description of the word "unconscious." It is on 24/7 and records in its database every form of sensory input that we allow in.

Our mind has a number of levels, distributed across Middle Self and Lower Self, each with specific duties to perform (see Figure 1):

- Conscious Rational Decision-making Mind, where we operate from if we are in control of our life
- Autopilot and Inner Middle Self, which house a number of sub-personalities

HIGH SELF
Connection to GOD Self. Akashic Record Telephone operator Connection to Source Mind and the Hall of Records

MIDDLE SELF
Conscious Rational Decision Making Mind Auto Pilot (Justifier, Judger sub-personalities) Inner Middle Self (Control, Manipulator sub- personalities) Instinctual Self, Survival Self

LOWER SELF
Subconscious Mind Ego Holographic Mind (Soul Mind)

Figure 1: Levels of the Mind

- Subconscious Mind, database or memory.
- Ego, or file manager that gets and puts data to and from Subconscious Mind

The challenge is to get all levels aligned with each other so they have the same objective and same priorities to accomplish our goals in life. But seldom do I find people with all four systems aligned and operating together.

The Middle Self

Middle Self consists of five components (see Figure 1):

- *Conscious Rational Decision-making Mind*, the functional aspect, the "keyboard" where you, the conscious self, program and control your life.
- *Conscious Mind Operating files:* The operating files that run your life on a day-to-day basis when you are in control of your mind's activities. If you are not in control, your mind goes on autopilot and Artificial Intelligence in Inner Middle Self.
- *Autopilot*, which can run your life without your control through Artificial Intelligence and all the sub-personalities in Middle Self's files. When people go on autopilot, they give their power away to a sub-personality that they created to escape from some situation or experience.
- *Inner Middle Self*, with Control and Manipulator sub-personalities: it will control all your behavior if you have given your personal power and control to autopilot. Artificial Intelligence (AI) is an operating system that operates through the inner mind's operating systems, and will control your life along with autopilot when you default on your attempt to regain control of your life and take your power back. It has an exact duplicate set of the file operating programs that are in

the Conscious Mind so it can run our life without our support.

- *Survival Self/Instinctual Mind,* which operates out of the limbic part of the brain. Some people describe it as the animal or reptilian mind. Brain researchers theorize that this is the oldest part of the brain. I feel this could be inaccurate since its actions interleave with the actions of the Inner Middle Self, which operates from beliefs, concepts, interpretations and attitudes. These, if acted on over time, will create programs and patterns. It also has a set of sub-personalities for each concept or belief. These two are not active unless one goes into survival from a life-threatening illness. Since the events of September 11, 2001, I have found 95% of my clients are operating out of Instinctual Mind. Apparently, most people found this event so traumatic that it disoriented and confused them, and caused them so much fear that they did not know whether they wanted to live or die. Very few people are aware that this happened, so they are unaware to this day that they're living in survival. You, the reader, may be in survival mode right now, and operating from Instinctual Mind files.

The committee in your Middle Self is also in session 24 hours a day. It doesn't care if you listen in, since it feels that it operates quite well without you. If you are not making the decisions that affect you and are not taking responsibility for what happens in your life, your sub-personalities will make the decisions for you.

They may not make the choices you would consciously make, but someone has to be at the helm all the time.

Autopilot and Artificial Intelligence may do a fine job of guiding you through your day if there are no crises or confrontations where you have to make decisions, but if a situation occurs that requires decisive action, someone has to make that decision. If you are not at the helm, your Inner Middle Self's irrational mind, your autopilot, and its committee will make your decisions for you.

Middle Self bases its action on how you have handled the situation in the past. It scans the files and, if no program exists, the committee will take whatever action best promotes its survival. If you are in a situation that, at a conscious level, you consider beneficial to you but which your committee of sub-personalities, along with the Amygdala Gland in your brain, views as threatening, it will try to sabotage you.

If you are not in total control of your life, your Middle Self committee will try to stop any threat to its power. If you give it the message that you are claiming your personal power and taking responsibility for your life, it will readily relinquish its power to you. However, at first, it won't trust you, and you will have to prove yourself.

If you have defaulted on attempts to reclaim your personal power and take control of your life, Artificial Intelligence, which operates out of Inner Conscious Mind, will have taken over control of your life with autopilot. At this point, you will need to demonstrate your intention and commitment, as Conscious Controlling Mind will not give up control easily if you have defaulted in many attempts to take control of your life.

The Operation of the Mind

The process begins with receipt of sensory input, be it a sound, sight, smell or touch. However, the stimulus can also be a thought or memory, meta-communication, information from higher sources, and new thought forms. Figure 2 shows how the mind routes information. Figures 3 and 4 show the results of the reactions and responses.

When our Conscious Mind records sensory input, it decides how it will react or respond, interprets how it feels about the incoming information, and places a feeling on it. It will either take responsi-

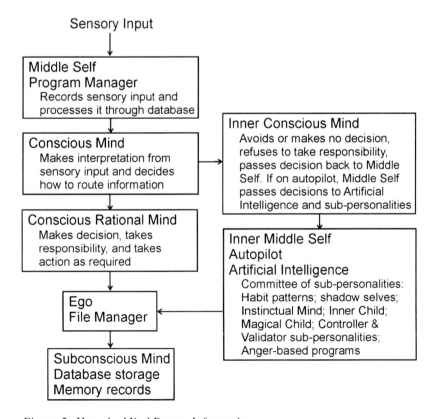

Figure 2: How the Mind Routes Information

bility and route the information to the Conscious Rational Mind, or make no decision and pass it on to Inner Conscious Mind and Middle Self. If we are making our own decisions on how to handle the situation, Middle Self routes the information to Ego (file manager), which files it in Subconscious Mind's database. Ego can retrieve information from our database and return it to Conscious Mind for future use.

As we can see by Figure 2, if we do not take responsibility, sensory input takes a totally different route through our mind. If we choose not to be in control, Artificial Intelligence runs our life quite well. The problem with this, however, is that we have no control about what action it takes. It could cause a stroke or heart attack to slow us down, or cause us to take notice of the people we are rejecting or avoiding. It can cause myriad illnesses and diseases to act out our fear or anger.

When we clear all the sub-personalities and the negative habit patterns, we can get control back. It takes some work to get the flow of information to run through our mind without being detoured through the sub-personalities. Figure 2 shows how the mind routes the sensory input through the operating systems and Figure 3a and 3b show how the mind responds or reacts to the sensory input and the effects it has on our behavior.

1. *Sensory input* (visual, auditory, physical feeling, meta-communication, and information from higher sources). and *new thought forms* (creative, inventive and intuitive), plus *processing dialogue* (negative or positive thought forms, flash back, memories, misinterpretations) are fed to the Middle Self.

2. *Middle Self interprets* the perceived information, processing through the Conscious Rational Mind or autopilot sub-personalities. (Middle Self and Subconscious Mind search for programs of past reactions or responses, and the operational program controls Reaction/Response.)

3. *Assignment of feeling:* Determines what action to take. At this point, you have two choices: Reaction or Response. Your choice is based on past belief or perceived effect from installed programs.

4. *Catalyst:* Loss of control pushes you into fear/anger, degenerating into emotional reaction and giving away your personal power.

5. *Unconscious Decision* is made in an instant based on Catalyst as to which action to take—flight or flight.

6. *Emotional Reaction:* No choice/ no decision, result in:
   a. *Flight/avoidance.* Run away from feeling;
   b. *Fight/confront.* Defensive, blowup out of control;
   c. *Defense of action.* Justification of action, denial feelings;
   d. *No reaction:* total avoidance with repression of feeling/emotion;
   e. Either *deny* or *wake up* to the lesson and review the situation that caused the reaction.

7. *Denial/Justification:* Falling back into the illusion of the past denial as a victim, justifying behavior as the only responsible reaction we could take. At this point, illusion and denial may form a denial-of-denial sub-personality, If this

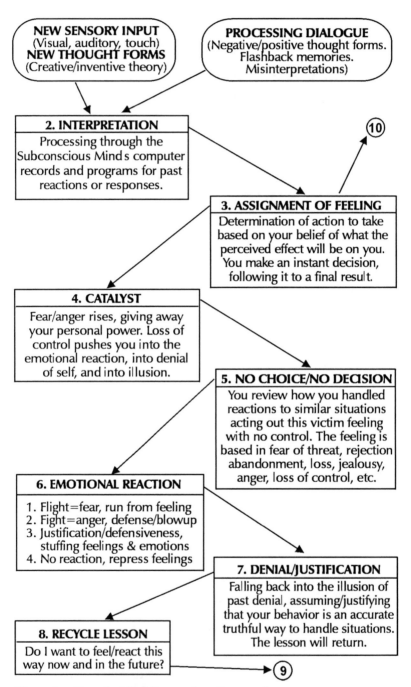

Figure 3a: How the Mind Responds to Sensory Input

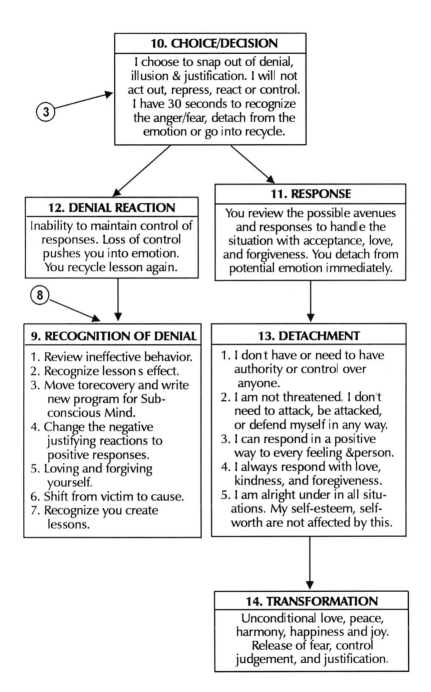

Figure 3b: How the Mind Responds to Sensory Input

happens, the cause of the behavior is totally suppressed *as if it does not exist.* We can then assume that our reaction was an accurate truthful way to handle the situation.

8. *Recycle Lesson:* At this point, you may review your behavior and ask yourself, "Do I want to feel/react this way now and in the future?" If you can do this, you can recycle the lesson.

9. *Recognition of Denial:*
    a. Review behavior you deem as ineffective;
    b. Recognize the effect of the lesson;
    c. Move into recovery and erase the ineffective program and remove the sub-personality driving the program;
    d. Remove denial-of-denial sub-personalities if you can recognize them;
    e. Change the negative justifying reactions to positive responses;
    f. Rewrite a new program and install it in the files;
    g. Recognize that you create all lessons, so that you can shift from victim to cause;
    h. Love and forgive yourself for allowing this to happen.

10. *Choice/Decision:* When we recognize this decision point, we have about 30 seconds to detach from the emotion and respond in an effective way. State, "I choose to step out of denial, illusion and justification. I will not act out, repress, justify, manipulate, try to control or judge another's behavior."

11. *Response:* If we are not able to detach from the emotion immediately, we will go into recycle. If we can respond effectively and positively, we review the possible avenues and responses to handle the situation with acceptance, forgiveness and unconditional love. At this point, we can detach from the emotion and avoid separation from self.

12. *Denial Reaction* will take over due to our inability to maintain and control our response. Loss of control will push us into the emotion. We recycle the lesson again.

13. *Detachment:* Hallmarks of successful detachment are the ability to recognize the feeling with a new viewpoint and interpretation, and honestly say to ourselves:

    a. This is not an attack on my self-worth or who I am.

    b. I do not have or need authority or control over anybody.

    c. I can respond in a positive manner to every feeling or situation and all people at all times.

    d. I am all right under all conditions, in all circumstances, in all situations and at all times.

    e. My self-esteem and self-worth are unaffected by this experience.

    f. I can respond with love, kindness and forgiveness at all times.

14. *Transformation:* This occurs when we can recognize that we do not need control or authority at any time. We will not be attacked at any time, nor do we have to defend ourselves or attack back. When we release fear, anger,

control, authority, judgment and justification, we have made
it through the transfiguration, and unconditional love, peace,
happiness, harmony and joy are our entitlement.

Split Personalities

Sub-personalities are the driving force behind habit patterns. If
you follow a certain action, belief or interpretation often
enough, it will become a habit pattern. If you deny that you
are following that pattern, it will become a denial sub-personality. If you persist in denying the program that the pattern created, you may become totally separated from yourself and move
into denial of denial. If you disassociate from yourself at times
of great stress, you become a split or multiple personality. At
this point, the sub-personalities become who you are, as you
become totally separated from self.

Most people with this dysfunction are labeled as psychotic or
schizophrenic, a condition that may result in a possessive spirit
walking in and taking over. At this point, people can leave for
short times (a few minutes to hours), but sometimes, people leave
for many years, with no recollection of what they have done or
where they have been. This demonstrates the awesome power of
the mind to operate without our approval or direction.

All mental dysfunction is caused by a choice by the mind to
create another world to run away from some traumatic experience.
Almost all dysfunction of this type starts with a childhood experience. The child will escape into an imaginary world that he or she
sets up to avoid pain. I refer to this as "escaping into the Magical
Child," which is controlled by the Inner Child sub-personality. This
will be carried through life until it released.

People can also disappear when they go on autopilot and give their power away to another created sub-personality that was created to escape from some situation or experience. Middle Self sub-personalities can set up autopilot operating systems in the Conscious Rational Mind and, as a result, our life is run without our consent or control.

Figure 4 portrays the formation of a split personality:

1. Sensory input from a trauma, pain, situation or any form of abuse will cause a person to escape into a magical child.

2. Middle Self creates a sub-personality to accommodate the escape.

3. Person goes on autopilot or has been on autopilot at times. This evolves into multiple sub-personalities that control the mind's functioning. The person and the original personality self shut down. Split personalities are a series of sub-personalities running a person's life.

4. Multiple personality disorder and schizophrenia are generally caused by an attached spirit-being taking over, becoming another personality self.

Summary of How the Mind Works

The brain is not the only part of the body that has the ability to think. Every cell has a limited ability to make decisions based on input by neuropeptides and cytokinins. Every organ and gland has receptors that communicate with the brain's switching network, and evaluate all sensory input as it comes in for interpretation for application.

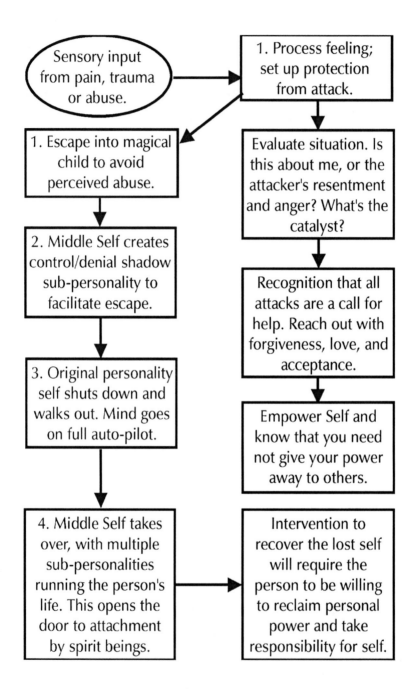

Figure 4: Creation of a Split Personality

The brain's switching network consults your mind's database for files from the past and decides how you will react or respond based on how you reacted in the past. Your mind interprets the feeling, which in turn causes a chemical reaction or response in the body at all levels. A positive feeling creates a positive response that sends supportive information to the cells, organs and glands, which in turn strengthens and builds health and wellness and a feeling of well-being. This feeling causes the release of the "happy" brain chemicals interlukins, seratonin, interferon, and L-Dopa, that in turn cause a feeling of peace, happiness, harmony, and joy.

Negative feelings, on the other hand, cause a chain reaction, shutting down the happy chemicals and sending negative reactions through the neuropeptides and cytokinins to the body at every level, which begins to suppress, depress and breakdown cellular structures in every cell, organ and gland. If the mind senses attack, it sets up a flight-or-flight syndrome. The immune and endocrine systems try to build a defense but are limited because they cannot counteract the negative thought form reaction that's being circulated throughout the body. The adrenals begin to pump all the time, creating adrenal overload as they try to support the body. The mind signals fear and stress, which cause the body to go into adrenal exhaustion trying to counteract the stress. If this continues to the point of adrenal exhaustion, it will cause depression.

If the Magical Child Syndrome is active and is triggered or activated, the personality self will shut down the Conscious Mind and disappear. Very seldom does one notice this happening as it is all internal. There is one exception to this reaction; those who are strong enough and have the willpower to stay in control can ward off the downer reaction for years. Eventually, the body will break down and the mind will crash the operating system, with traumatic results as the person will crash with depression or a serious illness.

Sub-personalities: Their Origin and Effect

Traditional Transactional Analysis works with five basic sub-personalities: Inner Child, Critical Parent, Survivor Self, Inner Adult, and Inner Self. These sub-personalities are the group that is in our mind's files from birth. They can have a major effect on your life and, if you operate on autopilot or give your power away to any of them, they will function *as you* and *for you*, projecting their agendas on your actions. Over the years, we discovered that the Personality Self is composed of more than 100 sub-personalities, along with all the mind's operating systems that drive them.

We have added another sub-personality to the basic five. Discovering the shadow self was another major breakthrough, for we discovered the sub-personality that creates conflict in our life. Shadow self works through and with Critical Parent, and focuses on criticism, negativity, anger, resentment, blame and rage, because it likes to stir up trouble, conflict and argument. Shadow self is the creator of compulsive/obsessive behavior patterns. It is also the cross-talker that is chattering in the back of our mind when we want to be quiet.

When we discovered that the mind is not limited to the basic five sub-personalities, we discovered that the Personality Self really runs our life, with its committee of 100 or more sub-personalities, each acting out a specific behavior trait. As we dug deeper into this, we discovered that Personality Self is what people have traditionally labeled Ego. As we expanded our knowledge of the concept, we found that we could change clients' personality traits, which changed their life path. People who were considered self-centered and egotistic would become more compassionate and supportive. Those who were nonassertive would move to a more assertive position and reclaim their personal power. Over time, we were able to show people how to reconstruct their personality so they would be more effective in their lives. This is the goal of psychology but it does not work very well. It certainly didn't work for me, so I gave it up and began to search for a new approach.

The five basic sub-personalities are indigenous to our mind. This means that they cannot be deleted or destroyed, even though I would like to have done so many times. We must train the basic sub-personalities to work with us, and give us control back. As children, we needed their help to navigate through life but, as we grew up and learned to deal with life, they should fade into the background. However, they do not "fade away" when people do not take their personal power back from them, preferring to relinquish responsibility for their life.

In the past, sub-personalities were believed to be located in the Subconscious Mind, but in fact, they reside in the Middle Self and function autonomously, almost as a separate mind. It was also thought that the five were driven by Ego, which spawned the term "egotistical" because they do, at times, display what most people mean by the term "egotistical behavior." However, this is erroneous because Ego has no driving force that would cause it to act egotistically, nor can it recreate a sub-personality trait that is driven by the

Controller, Justifier, Self-righteous, Competitor, Confronter, Know it all, Manipulator, Authority and Judger sub-personalities. The only part of mind that can create a sub-personality is Middle Self, which serves as Program Manager (see Figure 5).

When people are on autopilot, the sub-personalities run the body/mind on their own, having no real connection with Ego at all. The more we evaluated Ego, the more we found it to be simply a file manager for the database in Subconscious Mind's computer, serving as librarian, secretary, and file clerk. When we stopped

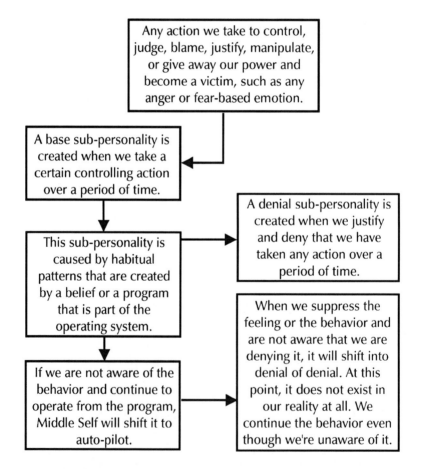

Figure 5: Creation of Sub-personalities

confronting Ego as an adversary, it became friendly and helpful. We also discovered an interesting phenomenon: people's memories started getting better, proving that Ego was the file clerk for our memory. As we delved into this vast unknown area of the mind, we found that the makeup of the mind was as orderly and smooth-running as a computer running an operating system and programs that could be reprogrammed.

We believed that Middle Self was the area of the mind in which sub-personalities operated; at least, that was our impression until we ran into autopilot, which has sub-personalities that we create when we let autopilot run our life and refuse to take responsibility. Although it resides in Middle Self, autopilot operates from the Conscious Mind working through Conscious Controlling Mind. We found many sub-personalities, each driving a particular emotion or behavioral habit pattern. We also found that sub-personalities can drive beliefs, interpretations, feelings and programs. The more we evaluated the Personality Self, the more we found that all emotional behavior is caused by sub-personalities. Programs cause emotional behavior, but they must have sub-personalities to act out the emotional behavior.

People often blame the Inner Child for unruly behavior, and then deny that they have control over it. Many people in 12-Step recovery groups such as Codependents Anonymous separate the Inner Child out as "not them" and then blame it for their emotional behavior. But Inner Child *is* part of us and we must get it to grow up and stop acting like a victim. The degree to which it will fight for control depends on how much power we have given to it. Most of the time, it is not working on its own but through the Magical Child Syndrome.

Survivor Self sees its role as protecting you, so it will sabotage you if it feels you are going the wrong direction. Critical Parent berates you for not doing an effective job, so that you reject yourself. Critical Parent is the most active in children because they feel they do not match up (due to rejection and parental expectations) and it spares no effort in validating any perceived shortcomings.

As you grow up, you create the Judger, Controller, Justifier, Manipulator, Competitor, Avoider and myriad anger and fear selves that run your life. And each time you run into a problem you cannot handle, your mind searches the database and may create another sub-personality to deal with it. If you encounter a habit pattern that you don't want to deal with and choose to delude yourself, your denial creates a denial sub-personality to justify your behavior and cover it up, so that you don't even understand what you are running away from. If you try to suppress the pattern totally, the sub-personality will create a "denial of denial" sub-personality to bury it completely. You will not even recognize the behavior pattern yet it is clearly visible to other people.

This cascade effect was one of the most significant causes of separation from self. When separation from self begins to take hold, an inner shadow sub-personality blocks the person from understanding this phenomena. The more we go into denial of separation from self, the more inner shadow sub-personalities are created. I have removed up to 35 inner shadow sub-personalities that were feeding negative self-talk to a client.

Sub-personalities can be up to three deep on any one subject. Not only that, but dysfunctional programs and patterns often have a backup sub-personality. If these are not addressed, they will create a new program or belief to drive them. We once believed that we simply had to get to the core issue and the base cause. Now we realize that we must also check for sub-personalities. That is not all; each sub-personality has denial sub-personalities, with a backup for each.

The hardest sub-personalities to locate are "denial of denial." Unless you're willing to face the truth and go for it, dropping all the illusions you operate from, and face the situations you are able to deal with, you cannot get to the denial sub-personalities. They are there for the very purpose of denial, so you will be blocked, making locating them very hard.

If you feel you have handled the situation when, in fact, all you did was suppress or release the feeling with a cathartic emotional discharge, then you put the issue into denial. The issue continues to be active except that it is suppressed and no longer accessible by your Conscious Mind. If the issue surfaces again and you do not clear it, then it goes into a "no perception of denial of denial" category, which means it has been locked in Denial files.

How the Mind Copes with Conflict

Figure 6 shows that we can deal with conflict in our lives in one of two ways:

a) Defensive and closed, which leads to the intent to protect against anticipated pain and fear, or

b) Non-defensively and open, with the intent to learn from the conflict.

With low self-esteem, and self-worth eroded by a negative environment, our primary motivation is the avoidance of future pain. We employ three main pain-avoidance strategies:

- *Compliance:* we comply out of fear of retribution and disapproval, which can lead to a "see-saw" of control behavior and retraction

- *Control:* we try to manipulate others by instilling guilt in them, as in "You'll be sorry when I'm dead or when I run away from home"

- *Indifference:* we withdraw, which can lead to sullen, unresponsive behavior.

In all three strategies, we develop mechanisms to cope with outer rejection and the negative consequences of our coping mechanisms, such as fighting with siblings, meaningless activities such as "hanging out," and appearing as though nothing matters.

On the other hand, with self-esteem and self-worth intact, we are eager to learn about the world and how we can best interact with it. We take responsibility for our actions and their conse-

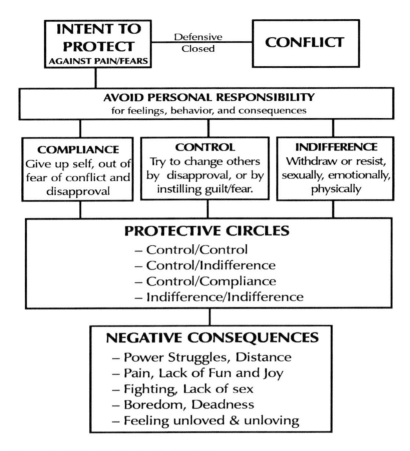

Figure 6a: How We Deal with Conflict

quences, seeing life as a learning experience. This leads to three main areas of exploration:

- Ourselves and other people, accepting any transitory pain that may result as part of the rich tapestry life.
- Why we and others act and feel as we do, and seeking the reasons behind what happens.
- Areas such as childhood, fears, expectations, and personal responsibility.

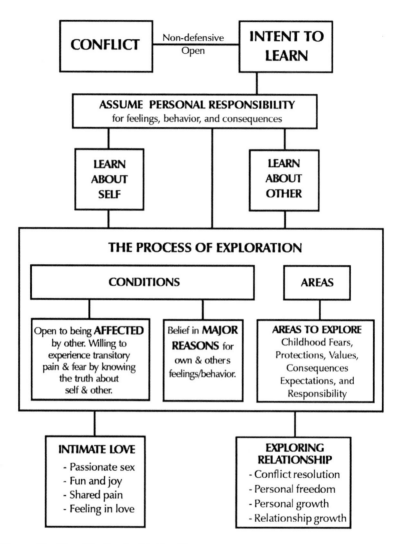

Figure 6b: How We Deal with Conflict

This openness leads to being able to share love in intimate relationships, accepting them as arenas in which to resolve conflicts and explore personal freedom, the overarching goals being growth of self, other, and the relationship.

Appendix C: Body Map

As Figures 1 and 2 show, fear is stored on the left side of the body; anger on the right, with rejection along the spine. In fact, we have uncovered sixty individual locations for specific other emotional, dysfunctional programs.

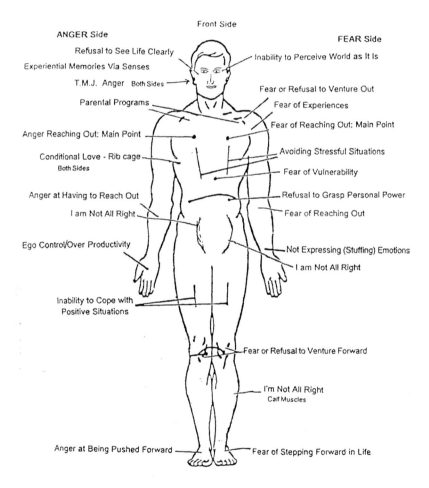

Figure 1: Body Map Front

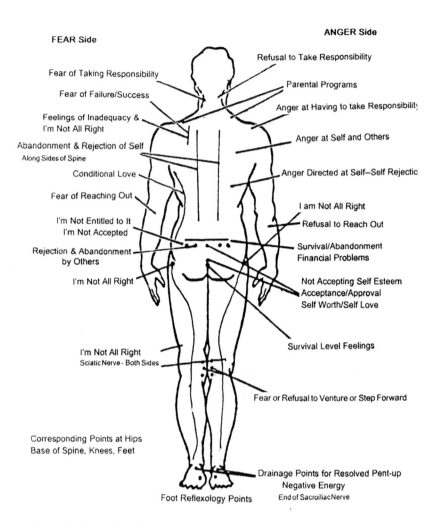

FEAR Side

ANGER Side

Refusal to Take Responsibility

Fear of Taking Responsibility

Parental Programs

Fear of Failure/Success

Anger at Having to take Responsibility

Feelings of Inadequacy &
I'm Not All Right

Anger at Self and Others

Abandonment & Rejection of Self
Along Sides of Spine

Conditional Love

Anger Directed at Self–Self Rejectio

Fear of Reaching Out

I am Not All Right

Refusal to Reach Out

I'm Not Entitled to It
I'm Not Accepted

Survival/Abandonment
Financial Problems

Rejection & Abandonment
by Others

I'm Not All Right

Not Accepting Self Esteem
Acceptance/Approval
Self Worth/Self Love

I'm Not All Right
Sciatic Nerve - Both Sides

Survival Level Feelings

Fear or Refusal to Venture or Step Forward

Corresponding Points at Hips
Base of Spine, Knees, Feet

Drainage Points for Resolved Pent-up
Negative Energy

Foot Reflexology Points

End of Sacroiliac Nerve

Figure 2: Body Map Back

Appendix D: Attitude Evaluation

Psychological/Mental/Emotional Attitude Evaluation

Score on a scale from one to ten on each question. Insert what you feel your value would be on a 1 to 10 scale. Your answer in each column does not have to add up to ten on each line. Go over the questions again using a pendulum or with Kinesiology to get what your Subconscious Mind's belief and interpretation are. You will find a major variation in the readings. The ideal is to get a 10 on all positive traits and zero on negative traits.

SET POINT ANALYSIS FOR _____ DATE: _____

General mental Attitudes and Feelings

1. I am not deserving ( )   I am deserving ( )
2. I am not worthy ( )   I am worthy ( )
3. I am not all Right ( )   I am all right ( )
4. I am not accepted ( )   I am accepted ( )
5. I need to be in control to be safe ( )   I am safe and secure in myself ( )
6. I am not able to trust myself ( )   I trust myself ( )
7. I do not recognize my value ( )   I have high dynamic value ( )
9. I need recognition ( )   People recognize my value ( )
12. My self-esteem is low ( )   My self-esteem is high ( )
13. My self-worth is low ( )   My self-worth is high ( )
14. My self-confidence is low ( )   My self-confidence is high ( )
15. I am working hard ( )   I am working in balance ( )
16. Life happens to me ( )   I create my life ( )
17. Others are to blame for causing   I draw all my lessons to me ( )
me to lose ( )
18. Life is full of conflicts and   I can handle the challenges before me
problems. ( )   ( )
19. I'm smaller than my problem ( )   I'm bigger than my challenges ( )
20. I have negative people around   I have positive people around me ( )
me ( )
21. I am closed to receiving ( )   I am open to receiving ( )
22. I think small ( )   I think big ( )
23. I focus on obstacles ( )   I focus on opportunities ( )
24. Fear stops me ( )   I work through fear ( )
25. I have to fight for everything ( )   Life Supports Me ( )
26. I have to suffer to get to success ( )   Success comes without strain ( )
27. I'm comfortable where I am ( )   I seek to grow and expand ( )
28. I don't like to talk about my feelings ( ) I can talk freely about how I feel ( )
29. I prefer to follow established rules ( )   I prefer to follow my own direction ( )
30. I have a hard time making decisions ( )   I make accurate immediate decisions ( )
31. I have a hard time taking   I am a "take control" person ( )
responsibility ( )
32. I am reserved and distant in   I am totally open and free in discussion
communication ( )   ( )
33. I am not able to trust my intuition ( )   I am able to trust my intuition ( )

34. I always stand in the background ( )   I am always in the front row ( )

35. I gravitate to the outside of the room ( )I gravitate to the center of the action ( )

36. I would rather analyze the situation ( ) I will take action now, see if it works ( )

36. My decisions are influenced by emotions ( )   Emotions do not affect my decisions ( )

37. I empathize with others feelings and trauma ( )   Others problems do not affect me ( )

38. I feel others situations personally ( )   I am compassionate, but don't get involved ( )

39. I like conventional practices ( )   I like new ideas and approaches ( )

40. I do not like criticism or judgment directed at me ( )   I am open to objective criticism ( )

41. I see myself as a failure ( )   I see myself as a successful person ( )

42. I see myself as mediocre ( )   I see myself as having value ( )

43. Life is a struggle ( )   Life is ease and flow ( )

44. I play to not lose ( )   I play to win ( )

45. I am sensitive to other people's opinions of me ( )   I value others honest opinions ( )

46. I am comfortable the way I am I do not need help( )   I always consider others' support ( )

47. I can make it on my own ( )   I will accept help from others ( )

48. If I ask for help, people will think I am weak ( )   I always ask for help if I need it ( )

49. I know all I need to know about life ( ) I am willing to learn and grow ( )5 0 . It does not bother me to leave things incomplete ( )   I like to complete my tasks ( )

51. I put things off rather settle them ( )   I complete tasks, communications ( ) 52. I have a hard time expressing my feelings ( )   I express myself without emotion ( )

53. I tell people what they want to hear ( )   I say what I want to say clearly ( )

55. I put off confronting issues ( )   I address issues directly and clearly ( )

56. I would rather do it myself than ask someone to do it and cause a conflict by forcing the issue ( )   If it is someone's responsibility, I ask them to take responsibility to do the task ( )

57. I usually have all the answers I need ( ) I am open to opinions and support ( )

58. I have resistance to authority ( )   I can be objective in a conflict ( )

59. I fear being placed in vulnerability ( )   I can be open and vulnerable ( )

60. I fear appearing inadequate ( )   I confront every issue clearly ( )

61. I feel isolated and alone in crowds ( )   I am happy with myself ( )

63. Fear overwhelms me, I cannot take control ( )   I am in control of my actions and feelings ( )

64. I recreate and live with my past ( )   I released the past, live in the present ( )

65. I feel insecure and unable to create a new reality( )   I create new opportunities everyday ( )

feelings and Attitudes about Money:

1. I do not deserve money ( )   I deserve money ( )
2. I want to be rich ( )   I am committed to being rich ( )
3. I unable to become rich ( )   I am qualified to be rich, I am attaining it now ( )
4. Money is the root of all evil ( )   Money isn't evil, but a vehicle of trade ( )
5. I don't feel good enough to be wealthy ( ) I feel good about becoming wealthy ( )
6. Money isn't important, I do without ( )   Becoming financially situated is important ( )
7. It is more enlightened to just exist ( )   Enlightened people can choose wealth ( )
8. Spiritual people not entitled to wealth ( ) Spiritual people are entitled to wealth ( )
9. You can't be spiritual and wealthy ( )   Most wealthy people are spiritual ( )
10. Getting rich is luck or fate ( )   Getting rich is easy if you follow the rules ( )
11. Getting rich isn't a skill to learn ( )   If you set the goal and the intention it's easy ( )
12. I do not want to spend the time it takes ( )   I am open to learning everything I can ( )
13. Never enough money for education ( )   I budget my educational funds so I can ( )
14. Success gurus charge too much ( )   I decide how much value I am receiving ( )
15. You must work hard for money ( )   I work smart, not hard ( )
16. I work only for money ( )   I work smart because it is satisfying ( )
17. I can't keep money when I get it ( )   I use my money effectively ( )
18. I don't want to struggle for money ( ) Money comes to me with ease   ( )
19. Money creates pain and anguish ( )   Money creates Joy and Happiness ( )
20. If I really tried to make money, I would fail so why try ( )   I always succeed at every task ( )
21. People will try to take my money ( )   I don't associate w/ unethical people ( )
22. I must control my money ( )   I can invest my funds. If I lose, I start over ( )
23. I am set for low income < $30k ( ) I am set for moderate income $100k ( )
24. Am set for high income > $300k + ( ) I am set for unlimited income ( )
25. I Am Set For Annual income of ( )   How much do you want? ( )
26. Saving money = scarcity ( )   Spending Money = Abundance ( )
27. Having money is responsibility ( )   Responsible people have money ( )
28. If I have wealth someone will have less ( )   My wealth has no effect on others ( )
29. I mismanage my money ( )   I am managing my money ( )
30. I pick losing investments ( )   I pick winning investments ( )
31. I have kow net worth ( )   I have moderate net worth ( )
32. I have high net worth ( )   I have unlimited net worth ( )
33. I am a business failure ( )   I am a business success ( )
34. I am an employee; I need a job ( )   I am an entrepreneur/owner ( )

35. I'm paid for my time ( )   I'm paid for my results ( )
36. My decisions are influenced by my   Emotions do not affect my decisions
emotions ( )   ( )
37. I empathize with others' feelings/   Others' problems do not affect me ( )
traumas ( )
38. I feel others' situations personally ( )   I am compassionate and don't get in-
                                           volved ( )
39. I like conventional practices ( )   I like new ideas and approaches ( )
40. People should only have as much   There is no limit the money you can
money as they need to live comfortably ( ) have ( )
41. I have potential for wealth,   I create my opportunities for wealth ( )
I just need a break ( )
42. Rich people did something bad or   Wealthy people earn their money
dishonest to get their wealth ( )   sharing and teaching others ( )
43. To be wealthy you have to use people
and take and advantage of them. ( )   Wealthy people provide employment
                                           for and contribute to the welfare of oth
                                           ers ( )
44. Money isn't really important ( )   Money is the vehicle that creates the
                                           economy ( )
45. I don't want to fight over money ( )   Balanced people don't fight over money
                                           ( )
46. When I get money people take it from   Wealthy people donate money to char
me ( )   ity ( )
47. Money is freedom, I can't handle   Money provides freedom if I handle it
it so I will never have freedom ( )   right ( )
48. Money can buy health, happiness ( )   Health and happiness are developed quali
                                           ties ( )
49. I don't have money, I never have   Money doesn't buy health, happiness ( )
happiness ( )
50. If you are rich in love, healthy and   Love and Happiness are desirable quali
happy you do not need a lot of money ( )   ties but they don't pay the bills. ( )
51. I do not want to be identified with   Many wealthy people are supportive car
wealthy, rich greedy people ( )   ing people. ( )
52. To help people I have to be one of   Wealthy people would rather pay
them ( )   others ( )
53. Chances are that if you're not born   It is not about birth, it is about desire,
into a rich family won't become rich ( )   drive, intention, commitment and disci
                                           pline ( )
54. Most of the good opportunities   We make create our own opportunities
are gone. ( )   ( )
55. You can't get rich doing with what   People get rich doing what they choose
you love ( )   ( )
56. As a women, it's hard to become rich ( )More women are becoming rich all the
                                           time ( )
57. Given my background it is difficult to We create our own opportunities by set
accumulate money and wealth ( )   ting goals and using our discipline to
                                           achieve them. ( )

58. I am always giving, but have a hard time receiving. I do not want to be indebted ( )

By giving and sharing I know I will re ceive a ten fold return. ( )

59. I do not have the time it takes to learn new ideas and concepts ( )

I am always learning new concepts, and applying them to my success ( )

60. Money is hard to hold onto. I always have more days than money ( )

My capacity to earn, learn, hold and grow financial resources expands every day. ( )

61. I wish I did not have to deal with money ( )

I deal with money effectively ( )

62. I'm not smart or intelligent enough to get rich ( )

All it takes is discipline and commitment ( )

63. Conventional values keep you safe ( )

I create my own set of values ( )

64. I find it hard to take risks ( )

The only way to succeed is to risk ( )

65. If I reach out too far, I'll fail ( )

I know no limits; I trust myself ( )

66. I am suspicious of people who offer to help ( )

I am open to support and help ( )

67. Success is an illusion in my life ( )

I'm committed to set my intention ( )

68. Goals never work for me so I never write them for fear that I will fail to achieve them. ( )

I set goals and follow through with In tention, commitment, drive and disci pline ( )

When I Was a Child, I Was Told:

1. "Money does not grow on trees." ( )
2. "Save your money for a rainy day you may need it." ( )
3. "We never have enough money so don't ask." ( )
4. "You must work hard for money." ( )
5. "You must be very careful and guard your money or you will lose it." ( )
6. "Money is freedom, but if you never have enough or never have freedom." ( )
7. "You better get a good education or you will never have any money." ( )
8. "Money does not buy happiness be satisfied with what you have." ( )
9. " Rich people are lucky; they get all the breaks." ( )
10. "We do not want to be identified with those greedy rich people."
11. "Rich people will take advantage of you be careful if you work or do business with them." ( )

Money represents to me
1. Anger ( )
2. Fear ( )
3. Pain ( )
4. Loss ( )
5. Anxiety ( )

I attain from having money:
1. Purpose ( )
2. Contribution ( )
3. Happiness ( )
4. Joy ( )
5. Peace ( )

Goals and Intentions on Physical Fitness: Diet, and Nutrition for optimum Health

1. I am committing myself to 20 minutes of exercise each day. ( )
2. I am setting my goal and intention to build up to one hour of exercise each day. ( )
3. (If you smoke) I am committed to stopping smoking now. ( )
4. I am committed to stopping consuming alcohol now. ( ) Occasional wine with meal accepted.
5. I am setting my intention to begin a new dietary program eating a nutritionally balanced diet. ( )
6. I am setting a goal to bring my weight into alignment with my perfect maintenance body weight. ( )
7. My body weight set point body is (_____).   My ideal set point for maintenance body weight is (_____).
8. I am willing to set up a dietary program that follows the best possible balanced program. ( )
9. I am committed to follow the Guidelines of Food Combining for perfect health ( )
10. My goal is to reverse the aging process to become younger. ( )
11. My chronological age is (_____) My physical body age is (_____)
Depending your physical health; diet/exercise, stress level and the toxic level of your body, your physical body age can be lower than your chronological age or older.

Recommendations for Proper Diet and Nutrition

Excess weight is epidemic today. Over 65% of the population is overweight, on the verge of obesity. Obesity in children has risen 300% in the last 20 years. Medical research and autopsies performed on young people under 25 years of age who have died from accidents, heart attacks, war casualties and other diseases reveal their physical bodies were equivalent to a person 50 to 60 years old. Cardiovascular blockages are as high as 50 to 80 %. This is the tragic effect of a junk food diet. It started about 45 years ago with advent of fast food restaurants.

To reduce weight, the body's thermogenesis must be working. This is the ability for the endocrine system to set up a process for the body to burn fat and oil. It controls metabolism and the body's heat factor which oxidizes and burns off excess carbohydrate build-up that causes excess weight. In overweight or obese people, it is shut down. The chemical response that allows the body to oxidize fat is turned off. The Chinese herb Mu Huang is the only ingredient that will reactivate the thermogenic process. Long, strenuous workouts over two hours and long-distance running will activate it through building up heat and activating the brain chemicals responsible for fat-burning . It makes no difference what diet or what exercise program you follow; you will not reduce your weight no matter how hard you try if your metabolism and thermogenesis are not functioning properly. We are working with a complex intricate computer that controls all the body's functions. It works well when it is operating correctly with programs in place. Our computer must have all programs operating correctly or the desired result will not be able to be reached. It is very easy to reset the weight maintenance set point with an affirmation.

Many researchers have claimed obese people are genetically set up or deficient in some areas which control metabolism. In reality, it is patterning that happens from family habits. If you set a pattern in your diet lacking in proper nutrients, it programs your body to set up your system to have slow metabolism and slow oxidizing of fat and carbohydrates. Overweight people tend to gravitate to foods that cause excess weight. All you have to do is observe people in a salad bar-style restaurant. Overweight people pick the high-carb food and eat very little of low-carb salads.

Another factor is lack of love. People from dysfunctional families who felt rejected, abandoned, abused or did not get love as children will gravitate toward sweets and high-carb food as it provides sugar which is a substitute for love. When they feel alone or rejected, they will go for food that satisfies the needy feeling. This builds a pattern that will begin to set up basic eating habits. If the parents have this pattern in place, they hand it down to their children. As a result their bodies then get patterned to desire the nutrient-lacking food. The body then begins to function and survive on sugar. It sets up a program to extract sugar from all the food we eat. When a person goes on a high-protein, low-carb, low-fat diet, it deprives the body of sugar so they are hungry all the time. When we reinstall the love program so they can love themselves and receive love, this craving goes away as the body no longer is needy for the love substitute. Since the thermogenesis is shut down and metabolism is slow, they have to be ungraded so they are functioning again.

To set up the weight reduction program, we have to check for the thermogenesis program and make sure it is not blocked by a program. Check metabolism and make sure it is not blocked by programs. Then we can delete and erase the current body weight-set point. We then reset the set-point for ideal body weight with an affirmation. If the lymph system is plugged up with toxins, we cannot get the garbage collector to remove toxins from the body. Most people are so toxic they need to do a six-week cleansing program. Once we get all the body's organs working properly, plus the programming set up properly, then weight loss will work well.

Suggestions to follow for perfect heath

1.   Check your urine pH (acid/alkaline balance) with litmus paper every morning. If it is below 6.5, then you need to

alkalyze your body. If it is down around 4.5, you are poisoning yourself with toxins.

2. Beef, lamb, pork and veal are very hard to digest. It takes digestive acid stronger than the acid in your car battery to digest. This can cause a build-up of toxins in the body due to incomplete digestion. Consuming empty carbs (white flour based food) and potatoes with heavy protein such as animal meat will cause the meat to putrefy and create toxins due to incomplete digestion.

3. Diets should contain up to 60% vegetables (preferably raw) no more than 20% protein and at least 20% fruit. Up to 20% of the vegetables can be interchanged with fruit.

4. Limit pre prepared foods from boxes and cans.

5. Eliminate frozen foods as much as possible.

6. Use fresh juices. Juices from concentrate, either frozen or bottled, are reduced to sugar and water when they are heated. The water is boiled off to make concentrate, so do not use.

7. It is preferable to eat vegetables as raw as possible. Heating above 100 degrees destroys all the enzyme value of the vegetables.

8. Oriental cooking is the most desirable form of cooking. Wok cooking uses flash heating and retains most food value. Make sure no MSG is used in preparation as it is very toxic.

9. Do not consume white flour products in any form, such as pasta, donuts, white bread, cakes, pastry, and tortillas. If you eat pasta or bread, etc., make sure it is 100% whole

grain with no enriched white flour. They must have the ingredients on the label. If you are on a well balanced diet, you can stray off it once in while with no negative effects, but do not justify this, as it will build a habit.

10. Do not eat carbohydrates with heavy protein as it will cause the protein to putrefy and not digest properly. Fish and some poultry are exceptions as they do not take strong acid to digest.

11. It would be in your best interest to eliminate animal protein from your diet. It causes toxins and has too much saturated fat. It also takes acid stronger than your battery acid to digest.

12. Do not eat foods preserved with nitrites, such as salami, pepperoni and similar types of meat, as they will change to nitrosomenes in our body and become very toxic.

13. Avoid chemical based foods such as fat free whipped cream which is just hydrogenated oil. Avoid soft serve ice cream which is fat free and has no milk products in it. It is not ice cream at all, but just chemicals!

14. Eat food in proper food combinations. Do not mix protein with fruit or any grain, nuts, bread or vegetables. This is a cardinal rule that cannot be violated. Eat fruit alone by itself. Exceptions are papaya and pineapple. They have digestive enzymes in them.

15. With food combinations properly set in our diet, our body can function at its highest level of effectiveness. If we mix incompatible foods, it breaks down because it cannot digest foods that are not compatible with each other. Many times we have heard people say, "I have

been eating this way for 40 years and I do not see any problem with my health." That may be true on the surface, but if we check the toxic level of the body and give a person a heavy stress test, we will find different results.

16. We are basically a grain, seed and vegetable eating species. We have a 32-foot-long digestive tract, which is the same as that of a goat. We can adjust to light protein such as fish and poultry. However, meat-eating animals have a 9-foot digestive tract, so meat passes through quickly and does not putrefy. Their digestive acid is so strong they can digest bones. Conversely, they cannot digest most grains and get much out of them, yet most dog foods are based on corn meal because it is inexpensive.

17. To understand food combinations, read the following books, and to get a clear understanding about food combinations, go to our book series *The Four Quadrants of Perfect Health*.

Suggested Reading List:

Herbert Shelton: *Food Combining Made Easy*
Harvey Diamond: *Food Combinations and Your Health*
Herman Ihara: *Acid Alkaline*

Contact information:

Energy Medicine Institute
916-663-9178
9936 Inwood Rd
Folsom, CA 95630
Email mailforart@gmail.com
Web site: www.energymedicineInstitute.com

For more information about Heather Forbes' books and CDs, her training and workshops:

The Beyond Consequences Institute (BCI) was created to educate and provide resources for helping children with severe acting out behaviors. Most traditional techniques accepted amongst nationally recognized professionals are fear-based and child-blaming. These techniques do not teach unconditional love and hence they send children into the world with corrupted and distorted love programs. The *Beyond Consequences* Parenting Model, based in love and scientific research, provides a simple yet powerful model for parents, even with the most difficult of children. Resources developed by Heather T. Forbes, LCSW are available at:

www.beyondconsequences.com

Appendix E: Medical Electronic Research
The StressBlocker™ [Patent Pending]

Disclaimer:

The following is a description of a unit used for research and testing. Due to FDA regulations, we make no claims as to what the StressBlocker will accomplish. We can only report what users have relayed to us. We check out the testimonials to find if we have multiple responses that verify the experiences people are having. Many claims have been made by users of the StressBlocker, but we cannot recommend it for anything as we are not psychiatrists or doctors. We are not allowed by law to diagnose or prescribe. We have come to a conclusion over the past ten years that based on the use by customers and these reports, the testimonials are accurate.

What Is the StressBlocker

The StressBlocker is small pocket-sized unit about the size of Blackberry cell phone. It has a radiated field 15 feet in diameter described as a Scalar Field which operates at 9.216 MHz. These fields are described in quantum physics as developed by Nikola Tesla, a contemporary of Thomas Edison. Tesla's field was electrical research.

The StressBlocker does not need to be placed or hooked up in any special location on your body. All you have to do is carry it in your pocket or purse. It should be carried 24/7 and kept within two feet of your body at all times for effective results. Some people can feel the energy immediately if they are sensitive to the energy. If you do not feel it, that does not mean the unit is not operating.

The flashing green light indicates the StressBlocker is working, and blinks every three seconds. The light flashes off when it is charging up the scalar field antenna, which takes three seconds, and then flashes on for three seconds as it discharges the scalar field. When light begins to dim, the StressBlocker needs to be recharged (see instructions below).

The StressBlocker Concept

This unit acts as both an ELF generator that radiates the earth resonance signal and a high frequency 9.216 MHz which is the ideal frequency for functioning of the body. The body/mind will intrain itself with the frequency that has the strongest effect on it. The StressBlocker creates a 15-foot diameter sphere of energy around the body, which causes the body to identify with this frequency level and block out other frequencies that are stressful to the body. All of the brain chemicals such as interlukens, serratonin, interferon, etc., operate at about 25 Hz. The immune and endocrine systems work more effectively when there is no load on the adrenal glands. The StressBlocker will activate and cause the endocrine system to rejenerate itself and become stronger and more effective to proect us from stress.

Tesla Theory and Technology

We asked some electronic wizards, radio frequency engineers and physicists why we were getting a clear AC sine wave coupled with a scalar wave without the circuitry to produce it. All they could say was that we are in hyper-dimensional physics and it was over their head. They could not explain it. One comment was, "You are into Tesla and Einstein's realm, and we do not understand what you are doing." We are apparently producing an output that no one understands. Nor has any history of this effect been recorded as far as we can see from our research.

The StressBlocker generates a bio-electrical magnetic field using electromagnetic scalar field technology developed by Nikola Tesla in the early 1900s. The coil-antennae produces a *Scalar Wave Field* described as a longitudinal wave field that functions outside of third-dimensional space/time. Since it operates outside of space time in our third dimensional world based on hyper-dimensional physics, it is unencumbered by the limitations of conventional physics rules. Scalar waves operate within the etheric field which surrounds the body.

When we shifted to the new unit, we were working with two new research consultants and a builder who was a project engineer. We now have on our team a radio frequency engineer and physicist. They seem to understand what we are working on and have offered suggestions on how to improve the StressBlocker. They have said, "It appears, as far as we can understand, that we are in at the threshold of a new discovery that has not been experienced in quantum physics at this time." They have not been able to measure the Scalar fields output, as it functions outside of conventional physical principles, but we have been able to measure the radio frequency which indicates it is the carrier wave field.

Operation of the StressBlocker – Electronic Medical Research

Every living being in the universe has a particular frequency that it resonates at when it is in perfect health. Each component of that being's body also resonates at a particular frequency. If the stress places conflict and disrupts this frequency, the particular cellular structure of the organ or gland is weakened and will be subject to breakdown, disease or illness The StressBlocker balances all the electrical, metabolic and electromagnetic systems that are dysfunctional, shutting out the disharmonious stress that causes the body to elevate its frequency. The device operates with fifth dimensional energy. It strengthens all the systems of the body by bringing down the frequency to the optimum level for perfect health.

To be in balance, most devices, plants and animals have positive and negative energies that rotate clockwise and counterclockwise. This creates a balance in the electrical system. A few plants such as garlic, onion, and some herbs radiate a double positive field, hence their antibiotic, healing qualities. The StressBlocker also radiates a double positive field, which explains the response it creates.

For more than 200 years of recorded history, the earth frequency or Schuman Resonance was 7.83 Hz. Recent research has shown it has risen to about 13.5 Hz. Our original Harmonizers were built at 7.83 Hz. We have been increasing the frequency in step with Schuman resonance. The body will identify with this frequency and resonate with this frequency blocking out other interference. When it is subjected to contact with the StressBlocker for a period of time, the body will duplicate the

StressBlocker frequency. It may take up to three days depending on the level at which your frequency has risen. When you are inside the 15-foot diameter bubble of the electromagnetic field, you will notice your body begin to slowdown and relax. When your body/mind resonates at this optimum level for a period of time, the body begins to heal. You may notice that the StressBlocker needs to be recharged more often than once a week in the beginning. If your body energy is low and you have been under considerable stress, this will draw the batteries down faster as the unit interfaces and responds to your body energy level. We have had reports that people having to charge the battery as often as every two days in the beginning.

StressBlocker Effect on the Body/Mind

Negative sensory input or negative thoughts and emotions cause the neuropeptides to cause the body's cellular structure to begin to break down. The same happens in the immune and endocrine systems, which causes them to lower their ability to protect us against stress and illness. The electrical field around the body must be strong to ward off disease factors. As the body frequency rises, the electrical and auric fields weaken. This electrical field is described as Chi, Ki or Prana. It gives a person more overall strength, vitality and protection.

The following is a greatly simplified explanation of the theory behind the StressBlocker. The information that causes the various parts of the body to operate is carried by the body's neurological network system. The brain serves as a "switching network center" that directs the information across the network to the appropriate parts of the body, with electrical impulses through the meridian system and with chemicals known as neuropeptides and cytikinins. These are all connected through a computer network from three levels of the mind. Each computer system networks with a mainframe computer known as the Inner Conscious Mind and the Subconscious Mind. The Subconscious mind acts as the database storage memory or hard disc for all programs and habit patterns. All three systems must work together or we will encounter malfunctions in the software that we describe as anger, fear, I am not all right, rejection, abandonment, resentment, need for control, manipulation and relationship conflicts. This causes breakdowns in the hardware which we describe as disease and illness or mental depression, etc.

Each cell is a mini-network computer that receives its orders from the mind through the neurological system. Electrolytes, neuropeptides, and cytokinins in the body are carriers. When operating properly, they maintain a delicate balance of chemicals, like the storage battery in your car. When they go out of balance or get run down, the electromagnetic fields breakdown. The result is your batteries are run down. The body loses its ability to protect itself properly. The ability for the brain/mind to communicate with the cellular computers breaks down and the body becomes subject to attack by diseases, illness and outside forces. When the physical body is in harmony, it functions at 25 Hz. However, stress and emotional conflict cause the internal frequency to rise to 7,500 Hz. When this happens, it becomes more difficult for neuropeptides, electrolytes, and the neurological system to transmit electrical impulses through the body/mind network. The rise in frequency causes all body tissues from the skin to the organs and endocrine system to be subject to stress, breakdown causing *accelerated aging.* This is the most damaging effect of increased stress and high frequency. The result is illness, depression, chronic fatigue, emotional instability and life-threatening disease. Metabolism is affected due to breakdown of the function of the endocrine glands as a result, nutrition supplied to the body slows down. Feeling tired and depleted causes chronic fatigue and depression is the result. As the internal frequency rises past 50 Hz, the good happy brain chemicals begin to shut down and the adrenals kick in larger doses of adrenaline to keep you functioning. The end result of this is adrenal insufficiency as the adrenals are overworked. They begin to produce less and less adrenaline, and when production drops to 20% or less, chronic fatigue begins set in. It is similar to low blood sugar caused by hypoglycemia that leads to diabetes but, high frequency causes breakdown in all systems of the body. The end result is Chronic Fatigue, Epstein-Bar or other forms of distress which leads to clinical depression. Many people run to the doctor and begin taking Prozac, Zantac, Zoloft, Valium, Paxil or other mind-altering drugs, described as anti-depressant drugs. You can get addicted to these feeling good drugs because they suppress the symptom and cause the brain switching network to believe the symptom of total body malfunction is a false message. The major dysfunction most people suffer from is adrenal exhaustion. When adrenal function drops below 20%, you go into adrenal exhaustion which is clinical depression in medical terms.

With the StressBlocker, the body can recover, bringing the frequency down, allowing the body to operate at 25 Hz. The adrenals can then heal and resume their normal operating level.

What Physical Effects Can You Expect?

These are only a few of the reported users. We have delivered over 2500 units, and the most often reported effects are clearing depression, lack of energy, and being able to slow down. Others have reported a much clearer mind and more vivid memory. People have experienced more clear and active meditations.

We have found it causes accelerated healing of cuts and wounds on the skin. It apparently is activating some cellular response, as skin cuts seem to heal in 10 times faster than normal. The unit is activating-supporting the immune and endocrine system. It seems to build up a persons immunity to illness. It is pushing up emotional programs that have been repressed in the past. There is only one negative aspect we have found – you have to deal with the suppressed feeling and programs that are forced up by the unit.

Now we find that it does much more than we expected. People are feeding back information to us now so we can report as we write a new brochure.

We hesitate to list results many people have received due to the fact that people tend to expect certain results from the StressBlocker as such many results might be placebo effects. It is an adjunct that responds with your body. You have to work with it; you cannot expect it to do things for you. Please do not put unrealistic expectations on the device. It can be a catalyst for miracles, and an adjunct for healing, but you must do your part in releasing your emotional trauma that is causing the results you experience. I t can have a placebo effect if you believe it works, and it works on almost anything. We can give others experiences such as many people have said that it pulled them out of depression in five days to two weeks without any drugs. Many have stopped using mind altering drugs. A two psychiatrists did validate this information from their experience with patients.

It causes accelerated healing by activating the cellular restructuring in the body to cause cellular regeneration at about ten times faster than the time it normally takes to heal. In my case, I took a chunk out of my foot with a chainsaw which was not healing very well. As soon as I had the new StressBlocker, my foot began to heal at a rate I had not seen before. The only way I can describe what I saw was like freeze-frame photography or watching it heal in slow motion daily. You could actually see it heal from one day to the next. The hole closed up and healed over in less than two weeks. The keloid scar caused by the gash is gone, all one can see is a red spot in the location of the wound. Generally in my experience, I have found that deep cuts like this one took many months to heal and they leave keloid scars that very seldom ever disappear. Most of my keloid scars have disappeared or smoothed over.

Are there any negative side effects?

We have been building and selling the StressBlocker under the names StressBuster, Harmonizer and Body/Mind Harmonizer for the last twelve years. There has not been one incident that has been reported to us of any negative effects on anyone who has used the units. As you can see from the testimonials above, everybody has had positive results. The few comments from people who have returned it have been that it did not work for them. What we have discovered was that at some level in their mind, they did not *want* it to work. We have found that the power of the mind can stop any positive effect if the person does not want to believe in the product or the process. It does not make any difference what it is or what can do for other people. *In a sense, we can state that belief controls everything so all results are a placebo effect since the mind controls the outcome of any, drug, supplement, product or therapy process.*

Background and History

With today's new computer technology and micro electronics, we have been able to reduce the size of the Tesla's original setup by 90%. We have refined the circuitry now the generation unit is much more efficient and uses much less battery current. Originally we used 9 volt batteries, and the unit used one a week which was quite expensive. We shifted to AA Nicad batteries but they have a charging memory, causing them to breakdown. We now use Nickel Metal Hydride batteries, and they have no charging memory plus they last up four years. The first prototype we built did not have a very strong field, yet it worked very well. We knew we were on to something so we continued our research. The production unit has a 800 millivolt output. The first unit of the current design had triple wound bifiler toroid ferrite iron core coil that was absorbing two thirds of the output. Our RF engineer suggested we use a plastic or a non-reactive ring. With more research, they suggested we go to a bar antennae. We discovered it put out three times the power in the field. There are no instruments to measure a scalar field at this time, but we can pick up the radio frequency.

Testimonials

1. It seems to bring programs to the surface which I did not have awareness of in the past. It is the best therapeutic tool I have come in contact with. *B.E. California*

2. I strapped the StressBlocker over a broken leg on the cast where the break was and the break healed four times faster. The doctor was amazed that we could take the cast off in less than four weeks. *J.S. California*

3. Chronic Fatigue that has been existing for years with no way out as it seems from past experience. It disappeared in less than a week. *J.C. Arizona*

4. I am feeling better as general well being and ability to handle stress more effectively. Not getting angry as easy as in the past. I left the StressBlocker home and I noticed my stress level began to rise at work. *C.D. California*

5. It has been reported to us by psychiatrists that have purchased the StressBlocker that it indeed does work with depression very well since it reactivates the brain chemicals and supports the rebuilding of normal production of all the essential brain chemicals allowing the adrenals to slow down and heal. As a result people seem to pull out of depression. *R.N. Virginia*

6. I put it on a plant that was seemingly dying. It revived in one day when the StressBlocker is placed next to them. *T.K. California*

7. A burn totally disappeared in three days. This was apparently caused by the activation of the cellular restructuring. *J.T. California*

8. It apparently has caused my immune system to recover because I am recovering from a long term illness that has

hung on from a long time. It is feels great to get my stamina back. *W.B. New Mexico*

9. It activates programs in the mind that have been covered up for years. Apparently denial programs are forced to the surface. *H.M. California*

10. I am finding I have more energy and I sleep less now that the stress is relieved. *G.B. Colorado*

11. I have been taking drugs for depression and low thyroid and adrenal function. I continued to take the drugs until they ran out. I noticed that I was getting the same effect from the StressBlocker so I did not renew my prescriptions. That was three years ago and I have not had any depression since. The new one is even better. Thank you so much. *AP California*

12. I handed the unit to friend of mine and he dropped it immediately. Said he could not hold onto it. I checked him and cleared him of attached beings and he had no problem holding it. *JOE. California*

13. I had been to the doctor for my high blood pressure and he suggested that I should be taking medicine to control my blood pressure because it was 190 over 120. I decided I would go back next month to check it again. It was still the same. I bought the StressBlocker and started carrying it with me all the time. I went to see the doctor again and my blood pressure was down to 120 over 80 in less than a month. The doctor felt the nurse had made a mistake, so he checked it himself with the same result. He could not understand how my blood pressure would come down to normal. His

statement was, "That just does not happen to someone your age.". I cannot attribute it to anything other than the StressBlocker. *CS Arizona*

14. It is amazing. I felt burned out and the doctor said my adrenals were very low and wanted me to take drugs to build them back up. I told him I did not take drugs of any kind. I would find a way to help me out. This is it. My adrenals recovered in three days. I do not feel as stressed out anymore. This is truly electronic medicine. *K.S. Oregon*

15. As a doctor working in an operating room almost every day, it can become very stressful. My stress level has been reduced to almost zero, and I also notice the people who work with me are operating under less stress. Everything goes like clockwork with no conflicts. *R.O. New Jersey*

16. My husband ended up with the cold/flu twice this winter and I usually get it from him and end up down for a week. This time no flu or anything. I can only assume the StressBlocker protected me and keep my immune system up to par so I was not affected. *C.H. California*

17. For me it is a miracle because I seem to go out of my body quite often. It is very dangerous for me to drive when this happens. I have been solidly in my body since I have been using the StressBlocker. *J.S. California*

18. I have had serious immune system problems for years. It seems that everything that comes along catches me. The StressBlocker has upgraded my Immune system to the point I am very seldom sick now. *C.K. California*

19. When I called to find out about the unit, I was willing to try anything as my blood pressure was 210 over 120 and I had lung congestion. My legs hurt so much I could not walk around the grocery store. In five weeks, my blood pressure went down to 130 over 90 and it continuing to go down. I have no lung congestion and I can drive trucks again. I have gone back to work full time. *H.N. Colorado*

20. I would not be without my StressBlocker because it protects me so well. I touch many clients in my work. In the past I was picking up spirit beings attaching to me from my clients. *J.N. California*

21. I have had low adrenal function almost all my life. Stress really take me down the point I cannot work. My downtime has been increasing too. With theStressBlocker, I have recovered totally. I have not experienced any depression or lack of energy since I have been using it. *C.K. Colorado*

22. Accelerated healing of burns has been amazing. I spilled boiling water on my face when I dropped a teakettle. The burn marks began clearing up in two weeks. In a month they were almost gone except for redness on the skin. There is no scaring as the burn marks are gone now. *MK. Arizona*

23. One of the most amazing sights I have seen is old burn scars and keeled scars are disappearing. Most of these have been on my body for 20 – 40 years. It is truly amazing. *H.M. California*

24. I finished a motorcycle race and took my protective leather clothing off and stepped into a serious third de-

gree burn from an exhaust pipe from a racing motorcycle. It must have been 1300 degrees when I brushed it with my leg. The burn healed in less than one month. In six weeks it just a was just a dark spot on my leg. In the past it has taken six months for burns like this to heal. *KG. California*

25. I have had panic attacks for 15 years and cannot drive in traffic. I am able to drive anytime now without taking medicine. *K.W.H. Pennsylvania*

26. I have been running at high speed, and the doctor told me to slow down. Being a workaholic, it was more stressful to push myself into slowing down which caused more problems The StressBlocker did it and I am back to normal.

27. I have been using psycho-active drugs for over 15 years or I go upside down emotionally. After using the StressBlocker for 4 weeks, I cut back on my drugs for two weeks until my prescription ran out. I have not taken drugs for two years now I feel great with more energy and happiness in my life. *Ivar, Washington*

Operating Instructions

> **Please read carefully before using the StressBlocker™**
> **If you are unsure or do not understand these instructions**
> **please contact the person who sold you the unit.**

The StressBlocker does not need to be placed, hooked up or set up in any special location. It operates 24/7. Carry it in your pocket or purse. It you set it down when you sleep, etc., keep it within two feet of your body at all times.

Some people can feel the energy of it immediately if they are sensitive to energy. If you do not feel it, that does not mean it is not working. For most people, it takes about two weeks to a month to notice a difference.

The green light will blink every three seconds. It indicates that the StressBlocker is working. It takes three second for the scalar field to charge the antennae, during which time the light is off. It then comes on for three seconds the scalar field discharges. When the light begins to dim, the unit should be recharged..

To charge: plug the charging unit into a 120v. outlet (the black unit with the plug) and plug the silver plug into the charging socket on the StressBlocker (the round socket next to the light).

If you purchased the Stationary StressBlocker, just plug it into a 120 v. AC outlet in your house or office. Try to center it in the building so it has maximum effect throughout the building.

IMPORTANT: On first receipt, plug in the charger for 6 hours as it is fully discharged prior to shipping. From then on, recharge 4 – 6 hours every two weeks, or when the green flashing light dims. We are using Nickel Metal Hydride batteries now as they have no memory. You can charge them any time but it takes longer to charge them. If the light goes out completely, you will need to recharge for a full eight hours. This is very important, as we have had people return the unit with the complaint that the battery was no good or would not charge. They had charged it with a cell phone charger of higher voltage and over-charged the battery for more than eight hours. *SO USE ONLY THE CHARGER SUPPLIED.*

Occasional overnight charges will not hurt the batteries but try to avoid long charge periods.

Be aware that the StressBlocker can and will activate programs or activities in your body. We've had people return units claiming it was making them sick. The StressBlocker has only positive effects, but can make you sick or feel down if you allow yourself to do so. If you have feelings start surfacing, make an effort to find out what they are and release them if possible. Split-personalities and subpersonalities can cause uneasiness if they feel they are losing control over you. Our intent is to get control over our mind so it will not work against us.

It is best to keep the StressBlocker within 2 feet of your body at all times, as it works as a bridge to balance your body. If you leave somewhere, check yourself out to see if you have attached beings on you as they see you as a target when you are using the StressBlocker. Generally after the first few days everything calms down and you will experience a sense of well being when your body slows down and operates at 12 – 25 Hz

New Products and Upgrades

1. The price of the portable 800 millivolt Body/Mind StressBlocker 9.216 MHz unit is **$297.00.** In Canada, price varies based on exchange rate which fluctuates.. In the US, add $10.00 shipping. In Canada, add approx. $15.00 – $30.00 USD. Shipping outside North America varies. (Older model Harmonizers can be exchanged for an updated StressBlocker for $100 – $150.00 depending on its age..

2. A new Stationary StressBlocker unit operates on 120v. for clearing offices and homes and creating an overall balancing/clearing effect in offices, houses, seminar and workshop facilities. We have been able to shield it so it will not affect TV and shortwave radio transmissions. The challenge is to build a stronger unit that will not interfere with reception. (We are close to having a unit here that could be classified as a portable radio station if we get any stronger. Then we would run into trouble with the FCC.)

Ordering

Order the StressBlocker via:

E-mail: Mailforart@gmail.com
Web Site: www.stressblocker.net
Phone: 916-663-9178
(We take PayPal on website orders and on phone orders.)

The StressBlocker has a lifetime warranty. Return it to us and we will repair it. We will repair any malfunction in the units at no charge if it is a breakdown in the unit. We charge for repairs for mishandling or damage caused by the user.

We will refund your money anytime within the first year of purchase if the unit is returned in good condition. However, we charge a $50.00 inspection fee to make sure we can resell the unit as a used product, plus the cost of any damage or repairs that may be needed to repair the unit, if their cost is over the $50.00 inspection fee.

.

CPSIA information can be obtained at www.ICGtesting.com
Printed in the USA
BVOW031805021212

307063BV00006B/16/P